# LEGENDS
## AND LORE
### OF THE
# NORTH SHORE

# LEGENDS AND LORE
## OF THE
# NORTH SHORE

PETER MUISE

THE
History
PRESS

Published by The History Press
Charleston, SC 29403
www.historypress.net

Copyright © 2014 by Peter Muise
All rights reserved

First published 2014

Manufactured in the United States

ISBN 978.1.62619.517.2

Library of Congress CIP data applied for.

# CONTENTS

# CONTENTS

# ACKNOWLEDGEMENTS

Special thanks to Lori Gilbert for choosing castles and cemeteries over the beach; to Onix Marrero for the occult symbols diagram; and to Stephen Shutt, David Goudsward and Donovan Louks for their help with the Lovecraft material. Thanks, of course, to my parents and brother for having strange reading material available when I was a kid, and especially to Tony Grima for keeping me grounded and being willing to go on some unusual daytrips.

# INTRODUCTION

There are lots of reasons to visit the towns and cities that stretch along the coast from Boston to New Hampshire. Quaint towns, interesting historic sites and sandy beaches draw tourists from around the world.

The North Shore is a beautiful part of Massachusetts, and many people are also proud to call it home. On any given day, parents are driving their kids to birthday parties, commuters are traveling to their jobs, high school teams are practicing for the next big game and retirees are hanging around Dunkin' Donuts.

In many ways, it's like any other part of America: orderly, safe, industrialized and rational. But just like every one of us, the North Shore has its irrational side—the side that's a little bit unusual, occasionally quirky and sometimes even scary.

This book is about that side of the North Shore: the witches who gathered at night, the pirates who buried their treasure on the beach, the abandoned and haunted places hidden in the woods and the bizarre humans and other creatures who have lived here. So take a step away from the rational world, at least for a while, and get acquainted with the strange and unusual heritage of the North Shore.

# Chapter 1

# NATIVE AMERICAN LORE AND MAGIC

The cities and towns that make up the North Shore are some of the oldest in the United States. Roger Conant founded Salem in 1626, only six years after the Pilgrims landed down on Cape Cod, and most other towns in the area were settled long before anyone even dreamt of the American Revolution. By American standards, the North Shore is almost ancient.

But it's important to remember that people lived here for thousands of years before the first Europeans ever set foot on the North Shore's beaches. Archaeologists believe the first humans came into Massachusetts more than ten thousand years ago. They were hunters and gatherers, and they followed mammoths, hairy bison and other game into the region as the animals grazed their way across the newly fertile landscape revealed by the retreat of the last ice age's glaciers.

Ten thousand years ago is ancient history by any standard. Although archaeologists have found tools and other artifacts from the ancient people who lived on the North Shore, very little is known about what they thought or how they lived.

For example, in the 1970s, several ancient Indian burials were discovered at Morrill's Point in Salisbury, Massachusetts. Some of the skeletons, many of which had been carefully buried in the fetal position, were more than five thousand years old. Intriguingly, the bodies had been ritually covered in red ochre, a pigment found in soil. The use of this pigment in burial rites indicates the deceased were part of the Red Paint culture, which existed along the New England, Canadian Maritime and Arctic coasts for thousands of years. Although archaeologists understand that the Red Paint people lived by fishing and hunting, they did not use writing, so we don't know anything about how they viewed the world. Their myths, legends and lore have been lost to us. The same holds true for the other ancient peoples who inhabited the area.

However, we do know a lot more about their descendants, the American Indians who inhabited the North Shore when the English explorers and settlers arrived. The tribes that inhabited the North Shore were known as the Pennacook, which means roughly "at the bottom of the hill." They are also sometimes referred to as the Pawtucket, which means "at the falls in the river."

For centuries, thousands of Pennacook lived in the area before they were killed by European diseases, for which they had no defense, and defeated in wars by the better-armed English. Their settlements were clustered near the ocean and rivers, which were convenient for both fishing and travel by canoe. The weather by the water was also conducive to growing crops like corn, squash and beans. An early Puritan settler in Salem, which was called *Naumkeag* by the Pennacook, noted the many "plains where there is much ground cleared by Indians" for their extensive gardens.

The Pennacook were divided into smaller tribes, each ruled over by a *sachem*, or chief. Sachems were usually men and passed their positions to their sons when they were no longer able to rule. Their rule was not autocratic and absolute but was instead based on how persuasive they were. Any of their subjects was free to give fealty to another sachem at any time.

While the sachems were the political leaders, the Pennacook sought spiritual and religious guidance from men called *powwows*. Although powwow is now used to mean a Native American gathering or celebration, it originally referred to someone who attained magical or spiritual power. It may be related to the word *taupowaw*, which meant one who spoke wisely. Powwows were shamans and worked with spirits to help the members of their tribes.

# MANITOUS AND SPIRITS

Like the other Indian groups in New England, the Pennacook believed everything in the world was infused with spiritual energy, which they called *manitou*. Trees, animals, rocks, rivers and people all possessed some degree of manitou. Some things contained a lot of it, such as large mountains or ancient trees. Unusual animals were also highly charged with manitou. Roger Williams, the founder of Rhode Island, wrote in 1643:

> *The Indians say they have black foxes, which they have often seene, but never could take any of them. They say they are Manittooes, that is Gods, Spirits, or Divine powers, as they say of everything which they cannot comprehend.*

Some people also possessed a lot of manitou. Williams noted, "Thus if they see one man excel others in Wisdom, Valour, Strength, Activity, etc. they cry out Manittoo."

The word manitou also referred to the many gods and spirits that inhabited the world. Like the other Algonquin tribes in New England, the Pennacook were polytheists, and many gods controlled the different aspects of the world. Although we don't know exactly how many gods the Pennacook worshipped, Roger Williams said the Narragansett of Rhode Island believed there were thirty-seven separate gods, and the Wampanoag on Martha's Vineyard believed the same.

The chief god was Cautantowwit, who lived in the southwest corner of the sky. If you're familiar with New England weather, you'll recognize that the

Roger Williams among the Narragansett Indians. *New York Public Library.*

most pleasant weather comes from this direction, so it's only fitting that the chief deity should live there. It was believed that Cautantowwit had created the first man and woman out of wood and had sent his messenger, the crow, to mankind bearing the gifts of corn and beans. He was also associated with the thunderbird, an enormous magical creature that brought thunder as it flew overhead. After death, the souls of the deceased would make their way to Cautantowwit's house, but the door would open only for those who had lived good lives. Those who had lived evilly were cursed to roam eternally.

Cautantowwit was mostly benevolent, but unfortunately he was not very responsive to the needs of mankind. He did not answer prayers, did not appear in dreams to give guidance and would send misfortune when he was unhappy with how people were acting. Fortunately, there were many other gods who did respond to the prayers and rituals of the powwows. These included the manitous that ruled over different aspects of the natural world, such as:

Wompanand: the Eastern God
Chekesuwand: the Western God
Wunnanameanit: the Northern God
Sowwand: the Southern God
Wetuomanit: the House God
Squauanit: the Woman's God
Muckquachuckquand: the Children's God
Keesuckquand: the Sun God
Nanepaushat: the Moon God
Paumpagussit: the Sea God
Yotaanit: the Fire God

Individuals would often take one particular god as their patron and believed that he or she watched over them.

The manitou that responded most often to human prayers and petitions was Hobbamock. Also known as Abbomacho, Cheepi and Chepian, this manitou was in many ways the opposite of Cautantowwit. Hobbamock was associated with the northeast, the direction from which the most unpleasant weather emanates. While Cautantowwit dwelt in the sky, Hobbamock could be found in the swamps, marshes and darkest forests. His sacred animal was the snake, and he controlled darkness and disease.

After reading this, you might think, "Hmm, that Hobbamock guy sure sounds like the Christian devil." The Puritans who settled in the area definitely thought he was, and they sometimes used his name when talking about the devil. It's important to point out that the Pennacook and other Algonquin tribes did not believe in the devil, however, and they did not view the spiritual world as being divided between forces of good and evil.

Each manitou controlled different aspects of the world, and if you wanted help in a certain area, you needed to work with the correct manitou. Since Hobbamock controlled disease, it was important for powwows to have a good relationship with him if they wanted to heal people. A man could not even become a powwow without seeing Hobbamock in a dream. Boston minister John Eliot asked several Indians how one became a powwow and was told that "if any of the Indians fall into a strange dreame wherein Chepian [aka Hobbamock] appeares unto them as a serpent, then the next day they tell the other Indians of it." Upon hearing about this dream, their neighbors "dance and rejoice…and so they become their Pawwaws."

After dreaming about Hobbamock, the new powwow would acquire various lesser manitous, which helped him in his work. For example, a powwow from Martha's Vineyard had four spirits he could summon. They appeared as a man who saw great distances, a crow that foretold trouble, a pigeon that gave wise advice and a serpent that healed and also harmed. These four manitous lived in different parts of his body.

One of the main functions of a powwow was to cure the sick. This was done by going into a trance and communicating with the helper spirits, which would diagnose the problem. Upon waking, the powwow often sucked the illness from the patient's body in the form of a small object like a stone or feather. The Pennacook and other Indians believed these disease-causing objects were shot into people by malevolent manitous, ghosts or angry powwows. William Wood, who lived in Lynn during the early 1600s, describes in his 1634 book, *New England's Prospect*, how a powwow healed a man who had a stick stuck in his foot:

> *A Pow-wow having a patient with the stump of some small tree run thorough his foot, being past the cure of his ordinary Surgery, betook himself to his charms, and being willing to show his miracle before the English stranger, he wrapped a piece of cloth about the foot of the lame man; upon that wrapping a Beaver skin, through which he laying his mouth to the Beaver skin, by his sucking charms he brought out the stump, which he spat into a tray of water, returning the foot as whole as its fellow in a short time.*

In other cases, a powwow would ask his spirits to lick the patient's wounds (invisible to all but the powwow himself), or he would concoct medicinal ointments from local herbs and plants. Naturally, the flip side of their ability to heal was that powwows also had the power to cause illness. This was accomplished by sending their spirits to attack an enemy or by stealing an enemy's soul while he dreamed.

# Passaconaway

Powwows had the ability to foretell the future and were often called on by sachems to give counsel. In some rare cases, spiritual power and political power were combined in a single individual, and sachems also served as powwows. This was the case with Passaconaway, a powerful Penacook powwow who ruled over the Merrimack River Valley as sachem in the 1600s. He was revered by other powwows as the most powerful shaman in all of New England, and as a sachem, his domain stretched from the mouth of the Merrimack River up into the White Mountains.

William Wood also recorded Passaconaway's magical feats: "If we may believe the Indians who report of one Passaconaway that he can make the water burn, the rocks move, the trees dance, metamorphize himself into a flaming man." In the winter, Passaconaway would burn a dead leaf to ashes, throw the ashes in water and then pull out a fresh new green leaf. He could also create a living snake from an empty snakeskin, which is quite fitting for someone who had a good relationship with Hobbamock.

A legend that appeared in the 1800s claims that as he neared death, Passaconaway mounted a sled pulled by wolves and headed north toward the White Mountains. They raced northward at incredible speed and eventually reached Mount Washington. Increasing their pace, the wolves pulled the sled faster and faster up the slopes of New England's highest mountain. When they reached the peak, the wolves raced rapidly down the other side, but Passaconaway was catapulted directly from the sled into the sky. He entered into the realm of Cautantowwit, where he remains today.

# Weetamoo and Winnepurkit

Another legend tells the story of Passaconaway's daughter, Weetamoo. She was loved by Winnepurkit, the sachem who ruled over the area that now includes Lynn, Saugus, Marblehead and Salem. He was an important sachem, and Passaconaway gave his permission for the two to wed.

An elaborate wedding was held at Passaconaway's home far to the north (near modern-day Concord, New Hampshire.) After the wedding, Winnepurkit and Weetamoo returned to Winnepurkit's home on the North Shore, accompanied by a band of Passaconaway's warriors. Another wedding celebration was held, and the two newlyweds lived happily for many months.

However, as time went by, Weetamoo grew homesick and told her husband she wanted to visit her father. Winnepurkit agreed, and Weetamoo traveled north to New Hampshire, this time accompanied by a band of Winnepurkit's warriors. After she arrived safely at her father's home, the warriors returned to the North Shore.

Weetamoo stayed with her father for many months, but eventually she missed her husband and told Passaconaway she was ready to return to Winnepurkit. Rather than send her south with a band of his warriors, the great sachem instead sent a single messenger to his son-in-law. His message was blunt: "Come and bring your wife home."

Winnepurkit took offense at being commanded by another sachem and sent word back to Passaconaway that he would not be sending any of his warriors to fetch Weetamoo. Instead, he suggested that his father-in-law send some of his own men with Weetamoo as an escort. Passaconaway, now also offended at being commanded by another sachem, refused.

Poor Weetamoo found herself stuck in the middle of this feud between two proud sachems. When she realized the dispute would not be resolved, she decided to take action herself. Traveling on foot from New Hampshire to Winnepurkit's home would take many days and was too dangerous for one woman to do alone, but traveling by water was faster and safer. One night, after her father had fallen asleep, Weetamoo crept quietly from Passaconaway's house to the banks of the Merrimack, stole a canoe and began paddling south toward her husband.

At first, the water was calm, but as she traveled through the night, it became rougher and rougher. Heavy rains and the spring thaw had thrown the river into flood mode, and as she approached some rough rapids, Weetamoo realized she had made a very bad decision.

The next morning, an empty canoe was found floating in the river. As the poet John Greenleaf Whittier wrote:

> *Down the white rapids like a sear leaf whirled,*
> *On the sharp rocks and piled-up ices hurled,*
> *Empty and broken, circled the canoe*
> *In the vexed pool below—but where was Weetamoo?*

Weetamoo was never seen again.

It's a poetic and tragic story about the price of being too proud, but if you don't like sad endings, you'll be happy to know that the earliest version of this story doesn't end with Weetamoo's death. It doesn't really have an ending at all.

The first version appears in a book written by Thomas Morton in 1637 called *New English Canaan*. Morton was an early Massachusetts settler who is probably most famous for raising a Maypole and angering the Pilgrims in Plymouth with his fun-loving lifestyle, but *New English Canaan* contains authentic accounts of Native American life. As far as Morton knew, Weetamoo didn't die but just remained stuck at her father's house. Unfortunately, the Pilgrims exiled Morton from Massachusetts in 1628, so he never learned how the dispute between the two sachems really ended.

However, historians do know what happened to Winnepurkit. Winnepurkit, whose name was also sometimes written as Winepoykin, had a very eventful life. He survived a smallpox plague in 1638 that killed his brother, fought with other local tribes against the English and was sold as a slave and sent to Barbados. He eventually made his way back to Massachusetts, where he died in 1684. Sometimes history is just as exciting as legend.

*Chapter 2*

# WITCHES AND WIZARDS OF THE NORTH SHORE

The English Puritans who colonized the North Shore differed from the local Indians in many ways, but they did have one thing in common: both groups believed in magic and the reality of the spirit world. But unlike their Indian neighbors, who thought magic could be used to help the community, the English generally viewed magic with great suspicion.

This split can be traced to the two groups' different views about the nature of divinity. The Algonquins of New England believed in many gods, but the Puritans were Christians and believed in only one single God. They felt God had a monopoly on spiritual power and magic. Anyone other than God who tried to use magic was going against God's will.

Since the Puritan leaders thought they were building God's kingdom on earth, social disorder was also seen as a threat to God's plan. The towns the English established along the North Shore were primarily small, close-knit communities where each person depended on his or her neighbor to survive. The success of each town depended on social harmony, and even minor disruptions to the social order like gossip or lying were a cause for concern.

## WITCHCRAFT BELIEFS

While on the surface all was harmonious in the Puritan towns, underneath the rigorously enforced social order were all the usual human interpersonal

An antique postcard showing a pillory and stocks used for punishment in Salem. *Boston Public Library.*

conflicts. Each misfortune, no matter how small, was viewed with suspicion. Why did one person's cow die but not his neighbor's? Why did one family's children become ill while another's remained healthy? Why didn't perfectly good milk churn properly into butter? Because open conflict was not approved of, the Puritans believed that many people used evil magic, or witchcraft, to secretly cause problems for neighbors they disliked. That kindly woman next door who smiled in the street and attended Sunday services might secretly be a malevolent witch.

Witches were believed to cause a wide range of problems. They made crops fail, summoned inclement weather, sank ships, sickened people and livestock and disrupted important household chores like weaving, butter churning and bread baking. Witches entered homes at night and rode sleeping men like horses until they were exhausted and sick; they also transformed themselves into animals to spy on neighbors. Witches also tormented the bodies of both humans and animals, causing them to behave strangely and contort in pain. At least, this is what the Puritans believed.

The Puritans thought the witches worked their evil magic in a variety of ways. Sometimes they created dolls in the image of their victims, which they could manipulate to cause pain or illness. Now often referred to as voodoo dolls, the dolls were called poppets in the seventeenth century. (Poppets have a long history and aren't particularly associated with Voodoo, an Afro-

20

This whimsical postcard hides the tragedy behind the Salem witch trials. *Boston Public Library.*

Caribbean religion, so the name voodoo doll is something of a misnomer.) In the 1690s, two men working in the basement of a house owned by Bridget Bishop found "several poppets made up of rags and hogs' bristles with headless pin in them with the points turned outward." These were used as evidence to convict and execute Bishop during the Salem witch trials. Candy, an African slave living in Salem, was also accused during the witch trials of making a poppet from rags. Unlike Bridget Bishop, Candy confessed to being a witch and escaped being hanged.

Although witches sometimes used physical tools like poppets, most often they sent their spirits out from their bodies to cause harm. The belief that some people can free their spirits from their bodies is an ancient one found in many cultures around the world. For example, the medieval Icelandic sagas tell of men and women who fall into trances and send their spirits out to gather information, while anthropologists studying in Siberia encountered shaman who sent their spirits from their bodies to heal the sick. The powwows of the North Shore had similar practices. The Puritan belief that witches used their spirits to work magic is just another version of this same belief, which is perhaps held across the world. Even today, some people talk about astral projection, which is simply a contemporary term for the same phenomenon.

However, unlike many other cultures, the Puritans thought witches did this only to cause evil. They called the witches' spirits specters, which even sounds sinister. While leaving their bodies safely at home, the witches' specters roamed across the community in human or animal form, visible or invisible, to terrorize their neighbors. Their specters also could invisibly disrupt household chores, inflict physical harm like bite marks or scratches on human victims and even possess the bodies of domestic animals and cause them to misbehave. Many witches also allegedly sent their spirits to mock and torment their victims while they slept.

Much like the Algonquin powwows, most witches had spirits that helped them. But while the Algonquin spirits could help heal people, the Puritans believed that a witch's helper spirits, called familiars, existed only to cause harm. Familiars appeared often as small animals like cats, birds and toads but sometimes also took strange, monstrous shapes. John Louder accused Bridget Bishop of harassing him with a familiar that had a human face, a monkey's body and the feet of a rooster. Sarah Osborne was accused during the Salem trials of possessing a familiar that was three feet high, humanoid and covered in long hair. It was believed that familiars fed by sucking blood from their master or mistress's body through small teats that looked like moles or pimples.

How did someone become a witch? Puritan ministers and theologians claimed that any individual could become a witch if he signed away his soul to the devil. During the Salem witch trials, the judges spent considerable effort pressuring the accused to admit they had entered into a compact with Satan. However, the average English colonist was more likely to think that witches were simply a part of life. Just as some people were tall or short, some people were just naturally witches.

The Puritan ministers and the common people also differed in their views about the morality of magic. To the Puritan theologians, any form of magic was an affront to God, and anyone who used magic even to work good was inadvertently working for the devil. Many common people, though, felt that magic was morally neutral and could be used for positive purposes. For example, ship captains and merchants often consulted astrologers to determine the best timing for a sea voyage. Unmarried young women would pour molten wax, hot lead or egg whites into a glass of water and interpret the shapes formed to determine the career or identity of a future husband.

The common people also used magic to defend themselves against witchcraft. Why not fight fire with fire? A horseshoe hung above the door or fresh bay leaves placed along the windows were believed to keep witches from entering the home. Boiling the urine of a sick person was believed to harm the witch who had caused the illness. Sometimes the sick person's urine was placed into a bottle with pins and nails and heated until the bottle exploded. (Don't try this at home!) Because witches sent their specters to cause illness in someone's body, it was believed there was a connection between the witch and the person they were harming. Causing harm to part of the sick person's body (i.e., their urine) would take advantage of the connection and injure the witch. This defensive magic was frowned on by the Puritan ministers.

## ELIZABETH MORSE AND CALEB POWELL: WITCHCRAFT IN OLD NEWBURY

Although the Salem trials are the most famous of their kind, there were other witchcraft trials on the North Shore before them. For example, in 1651, John Bradstreet of Rowley was accused of having familiarity with the devil and bewitching a dog. During his trial, he confessed to having a magic book and hearing a voice that told him to build a bridge of sand over the sea and a bridge up to heaven. Bradstreet was whipped for lying and having "fanciful delusions." The bewitched dog did not get off so lightly and was unfortunately hanged.

Other trials followed after John Bradstreet's. In 1670, Ann Burt of Lynn was accused of witchcraft, as was Bridget Oliver of Salem in 1680. Neither was found guilty.

Elizabeth Morse of Newbury was not so lucky. In 1680, this elderly woman was found guilty of witchcraft and sentenced to death.

Elizabeth Morse and her husband, William, a shoemaker, lived in a small house on Market Street in Newbury. This part of old Newbury is now Newburyport, and the Morse house was near what is now St. Paul's Church on High Street. The Morses lived together with their grandson, John Stiles.

In the fall of 1679, the Morse household began to be afflicted with strange happenings. Sticks and stones were thrown against the house in the middle of the night, but no one could be seen throwing them. One of the family's hogs mysteriously appeared inside the house one night at midnight when all the doors were locked. A basket was thrown down the chimney, but when William took the basket and laid it on a table, it disappeared and came down the chimney once more. An andiron from the fireplace danced across the table and knocked over a soup pot.

But these strange phenomena were just minor inconveniences compared to the violent physical attacks against Elizabeth and William. During the trial, William said:

> *My wife came out of the other room, a wedge of iron being thrown at her, and a spade, but did not reach her, and a stone, which hurt her much…A shoe, which we saw in the chamber before came down the chimney, the door being shut, and struck me a blow on the head which did much hurt.*

Their grandson also was afflicted. John suffered from strange fits and seizures, and at night, he said his bed jumped up and down. The local doctor was summoned but could not diagnose a physical ailment. It seemed likely the cause was supernatural. Elizabeth Morse was not popular with her neighbors, and people began to mutter that she was a witch and had bewitched her own home.

Caleb Powell, a sailor and friend of the family who lived nearby, offered his help to the Morses. As William said during the trial:

> [Powell] *said he much grieved for me and said the boy was the cause of all my trouble and my wife was much wronged and was no witch, and if I would let him have the boy but one day he would warrant me no more trouble. I being persuaded to it he came the next day at the break of day, and the boy was with him until night and I had not any trouble since.*

William and Elizabeth were not convinced by the sailor's story. Instead, they thought that if Caleb Powell was able to stop the strange phenomena, then he must have been the person who had caused it in the first place. Therefore, in their minds, Caleb Powell was the witch. They went to the authorities with their suspicions and had Powell arrested on December 8, 1679.

Several people testified against Powell at his trial. A woman named Elizabeth Titcomb said Powell had been brought up by a wizard in Gloucester named Francis Norwood, who had studied the black arts. One John Badger claimed Powell knew astrology and astronomy, while William Morse said Powell knew the "working of spirits, some in one country and some in another." The boatswain of Powell's ship reputedly said, "If there were any wizards he was sure Caleb Powell was one."

Things didn't look good for Caleb Powell, but when he took the stand, he offered a mundane explanation for what had been happening in the Morse household. He said that one day when he was walking by their house, he stopped and looked in the window. Inside, he saw William Morse sitting at prayer with his eyes closed. A moment later, his grandson, John, entered the room and threw a shoe at the old man's head. There was no witchcraft involved, Powell argued, just a mischievous boy playing pranks. This was why the uncanny activities stopped once he removed John from the house.

The court set Caleb Powell free in February 1680. The judges didn't acquit him but instead said he "justly deserves to bear his own shame and the costs of prosecution of the complaint." Apparently, they didn't think he was bewitching the Morse household, but they still suspected he was dabbling in magic.

Although Caleb Powell was happy to be free, the people of Newbury weren't pleased with the judges' decision. They knew some witch must be responsible, so they came forth with their original suspicion and accused Elizabeth Morse of bewitching her own household.

The authorities arrested Elizabeth and put her on trial. Elizabeth Morse was argumentative, a personality trait that had not endeared her to the citizens of Newbury. Seventeen neighbors came forward to testify against her, airing petty complaints and grievances that went back a dozen years.

Many of the accusations involved livestock. One neighbor said that after he argued with Elizabeth, his cow would not nurse its own calf. Sheep also wandered mysteriously onto the Morses' property—clearly she was trying to steal them through witchcraft. Zechariah Davis of Salisbury testified that after he argued with Elizabeth Morse over some fowl, one of his calves "danced and roared" and then "was sitting upon his tail like a dog, and I never see no calf sit after that manner before." The calf died shortly thereafter.

John Chase testified that Elizabeth Morse had entered his bedroom through a tiny hole one night, while another man claimed he saw half her body walking around during the daytime. Clearly, Elizabeth had been sending out her specter to terrorize the town. James Browne claimed that a bruise appeared on Elizabeth's leg in the same spot where he struck a cat that was pestering him, implying that the cat had really been Elizabeth's spirit in feline form.

Most seriously of all, once when Elizabeth saw a sick child, she told its mother she thought it might die. The child died soon afterward, and its mother accused Elizabeth of murdering it through magic. Elizabeth was also accused of killing one Goodwife Chandler. (Goodwife was a title used for married women, similar to our modern term "Mrs.") Goodwife Chandler had become ill shortly after a visit from Elizabeth Morse and suspected she had been bewitched. She nailed a horseshoe over her door to keep Morse out, which seemed to work until one of her more pious neighbors took it down, saying that even defensive magic was the devil's work. Elizabeth Morse came to visit again, and Goody Chandler died soon after.

Although all this testimony sounds like gossip and coincidence to a modern reader, the judges felt otherwise. They were convinced Elizabeth Morse was a witch and sentenced her to death. The execution order was never carried out. Although the historical records are a little unclear, it seems that she got a reprieve from the governor, and her sentence was reduced to house arrest. She spent the remainder of her short life confined to her home. The stress of the trial and the harsh jail conditions had ruined her health, and she died after only a few years. Her grandson, John Stiles, who probably was the cause of all her problems, escaped any punishment.

# THE SALEM WITCH TRIALS: THE WITCH HUNT BEGINS

The North Shore experienced a few years without any significant witchcraft trials after Elizabeth Morse's conviction, although in 1685, Bridget Oliver of Salem was accused of killing her husband with magic. This was an isolated incident, and she was acquitted, but it indicates that fear of witchcraft still lurked within Puritan society. It was just waiting for the right spark to ignite into a full-fledged witch hunt.

The early 1690s presented just the right conditions because, by that decade, the Massachusetts Bay Colony was in a state of upheaval. The new king in England had revoked the colony's original charter, and the colonists wondered nervously about the future of their settlements. Adding to the confusion, French soldiers from Canada and their Indian allies had begun attacking the colony's northernmost frontier in the areas we now know as Maine and New Hampshire. Villages were burned and pillaged, English settlers were killed or made captive and hordes of refugees fled to coastal Massachusetts seeking safety. As they crowded into towns like Salem, they told tales of violence and warfare. The Puritan ministers decreed that the political chaos was the work of Satan.

In the town of Salem, the colony's upheaval was mirrored at the local level. Salem was split by internal conflict. The settlement was officially divided into two parts: the wealthy coastal port of Salem Town (now the city of Salem) and the rural inland farming community of Salem Village (now the city of Danvers). Salem Village was subordinate to Salem Town in political and religious matters, and its residents were divided on whether to seek independence for their community.

The fear and confusion transformed into a witch hunt in the winter of 1692. Reverend Samuel Parris of Salem Village noticed that his nine-year-old daughter, Betty, and her cousin Abigail Williams, a refugee orphaned in an Indian raid, were behaving very oddly. They contorted their bodies into bizarre and painful positions, made animalistic sounds and attempted to climb up the chimney. At other times, they were paralyzed with fear or felt sharp pains through their bodies. Throughout January and February, Reverend Parris and his wife tried various homemade remedies, including parsnip seeds soaked in wine and castor oil mixed with amber. Nothing worked. The local physician, Dr. Samuel Griggs, could find no physical cause for their ailments. Eight other girls and young women in Salem Village began to exhibit similar behavior. People began to mutter that perhaps the girls were bewitched.

Mary Sibley, an aunt of one of the bewitched girls, instructed Reverend Parris's slave Tituba to make a cake out of flour and urine from one of the bewitched girls. The cake was then fed to a dog. This was a simple form of magic designed to diagnose witchcraft. The belief was that if the girls were bewitched, their urine should be bewitched as well. If the dog became

The Salem Witch House, still standing today, was the home of trial judge Jonathan Corwin. *Boston Public Library.*

bewitched after eating the urine cake, it would prove a witch was causing the girls' problems.

Although history doesn't record the result of Mary Sibley's spell, we do know Reverend Parris's reaction. He was furious. Puritan ministers thought all magic came from Satan, and he publicly accused her of "going to the Devil for help with the Devil." She tearfully signed a public apology during Sunday meeting, but the people of Salem Village agreed with Mary Sibley. Their community was under attack from witches, and something had to be done about it. The colony's government created a special court, called the Court of Oyer and Terminer, to investigate. "Oyer and Terminer" is an old legal term meaning "to hear and determine."

The afflicted girls at first accused only 3 people (including Tituba) of witchcraft, but over the course of 1692, the number grew to more than 150. The accused came not only from Salem Town and Salem Village but also from across the North Shore and many other parts of New England, including Boston, Maine and New Hampshire. The number of afflicted grew to more than 70, primarily girls and young women. Women also made up the majority of those accused of witchcraft, but some men were both accused and afflicted as well.

# THE SALEM WITCH TRIALS:
## SPECTRAL EVIDENCE AND NINETEEN EXECUTIONS

The Puritans believed witches used their specters to commit most of their crimes, but their specters were usually invisible except to the witches and their victims. This meant witchcraft was a crime that created little hard evidence that could be produced in court. Because of this, the judges relied on "spectral evidence" to convict witches. Spectral evidence most often took the form of dreams or visions that an afflicted person had of an alleged witch. For example, if someone claimed a witch had entered his bedroom at night in the form of a black cat, the judges would accept this as valid evidence, even though it sounds suspiciously like a dream.

During the trials, the afflicted people even claimed the witches' specters were invisibly tormenting them in the courtroom. The judges also accepted these visions as valid evidence, even though the accused witches were usually seated in plain sight and heavily guarded. It was believed that an afflicted person's torments would stop if they simply touched the

The afflicted girls point at spectral evidence visible only to them. *New York Public Library.*

witch who was causing them pain, and the judges also admitted the touch test as valid evidence.

Based almost entirely on spectral evidence and gossip, nineteen people were found guilty and hanged for the crime of witchcraft. They were:

Bridget Bishop: After being acquitted of witchcraft in the death of her husband at an earlier trial in 1685, Bridget Oliver married a wealthy Beverly man named Edward Bishop and took his name. The afflicted girls accused her of sending her specter to physically torment them and tempt them to sign the devil's book.

Reverend George Burroughs: A former minister of Salem Village, Burroughs was living in Maine when the trials started. He was accused of exhibiting supernatural strength and being the head of the witches attacking Salem. The ghosts of his dead wives appeared to the afflicted girls and told them Burroughs had murdered them. As he stood on Gallows Hill waiting to be hanged, he successfully recited the Lord's Prayer, something it was said no witch could do. The crowd gathered for his execution grew doubtful, but the afflicted said they saw the devil whispering the prayer into his ear, and he was hanged.

Martha Carrier: The Carrier family was quite poor, and after being suspected of spreading smallpox, they lived on the outskirts of Andover as pariahs. Martha Carrier was accused of flying in spirit to the witches' meeting, held invisibly in the pasture near Reverend Parris's house, where she partook of unholy sacraments administered by Reverend Burroughs. The afflicted girls claimed Satan had promised Martha Carrier she would be the Queen of Hell if she tormented them with great pain.

Martha Corey: A self-proclaimed "Gospel Woman," Martha Corey was an argumentative member of Salem Village's church, where she regularly attended Sunday meeting. People said she had an uncanny way of knowing what they were about to say, and even her husband, Giles, suspected she was a witch. When she attended Sunday meeting, the afflicted girls present contorted in pain and claimed they saw her specter mocking them from the rafters.

Mary Esty: When Mary Esty, the sister of respected community member Rebecca Nurse, was brought in front of the afflicted, they found themselves compelled to copy every movement of her body. When she bent her neck, theirs snapped downward, suddenly in pain. When she put her hands together, their hands became stuck together and couldn't be pulled apart. They also claimed she had brought them the devil's book to sign.

Sarah Good: One of the first to be accused of witchcraft, Sarah Good was poor and foul tempered. If neighbors refused to give her what she

A nineteenth-century illustration of the trial of Reverend George Burroughs. *Library of Congress, Prints and Photographs Division.*

begged for, she cursed them under her breath. She was accused of being served by multiple familiars, including cats and a yellow bird that fed on her blood. According to legend, before she was hanged, she issued one last curse, telling Salem's Reverend Nicholas Noyes, "I am no more a witch than you are a wizard, and if you take away my life God will give you blood to drink." When Reverend Noyes died of a brain hemorrhage several years later, his neighbors said blood gushed from his mouth, fulfilling the curse. Sarah Good's five-year-old daughter, Dorcas, was imprisoned during the witchcraft trials but was not executed.

ELIZABETH HOW: A resident of Topsfield, Elizabeth How was accused of bewitching people both there and in Salem Village. When she had petitioned to join the Ipswich church a few years earlier, the livestock of people who opposed her membership sickened and died, and during her trial, Elizabeth How's very glance caused the afflicted to feel pain. Although the ministers from Ipswich vouched that she was no witch, she was still found guilty and executed.

GEORGE JACOBS SR.: Multiple people accused seventy-year-old George Jacobs Sr. of being a witch, including his granddaughter Margaret. Margaret herself had been accused earlier, and to avoid the gallows, she pleaded guilty. When pressured by the magistrates, she named her grandfather and several

The grave of George Jacobs Sr. in Danvers. *Photo by author.*

others as witches. She later recanted her confession, but it was too late for George, who was hanged on August 16, 1692. Before dying, he forgave his granddaughter and left her silver coins in his will.

SUSANNAH MARTIN: An argumentative widow from Amesbury, Susannah Martin had been suspected of witchcraft for decades. When she appeared in court, she laughed at the antics of the afflicted and argued that since the devil could take any form, perhaps he was assuming her shape to afflict the people of Salem. When the afflicted tried to touch her to calm their torments, they were thrown to the ground by an invisible force.

REBECCA NURSE: In her seventies, bedridden and a respected member of the community, Rebecca Nurse was nonetheless accused, found guilty and hanged. Those who were executed for witchcraft were buried in unmarked and unhallowed graves on Gallows Hill in Salem, but Rebecca's family stole her body by night and brought it to the family farm in Salem Village, where they reburied it. A large monument now marks the spot at the historic Rebecca Nurse Homestead in Danvers. George Jacobs Sr. is also now buried at the same site.

ALICE PARKER: Alice Parker was the wife of a Salem fisherman and suffered from fits, possibly epileptic in nature. One Salem man claimed he

The Rebecca Nurse homestead in Danvers. *Library of Congress, Prints and Photographs Division.*

had been chased across Salem common by her specter, while Mary Warren of Salem Village claimed her mother had died after her father failed to mow Alice Parker's hay as he had promised. Mary's tongue protruded from her mouth and turned black while Alice was testifying, to which Alice snapped, "Her tongue will be blacker before she dies." After saying this, she was sent with other suspects to Boston's jail before being hanged.

MARY PARKER: When Mary Parker, a wealthy widow from Andover, was brought into the court, several afflicted girls immediately began convulsing. Mary Warren convulsed so violently that she bled from her mouth, and a pin mysteriously was found stuck into her hand. Mary Parker asked if the girls were confusing her with her sister-in-law who had the same name, but their torments stopped when they touched her— proof that she was the bewitcher.

JOHN PROCTOR: Now famous as the main character in Arthur Miller's play *The Crucible*, Proctor was a Salem Village farmer with a reputation as a violent disciplinarian. His servant girl, Mary Warren, was one of the afflicted girls, but Proctor threatened to beat her if she had any more fits. Proctor also threatened to beat the devil out of Tituba's husband, John Indian, when he accused Proctor's wife of witchcraft. The afflicted soon saw his specter moving through the court causing them pain, and he was found guilty of witchcraft himself.

ANN PUDEATOR: Twice widowed and a former resident of Maine, Anne Pudeator lived in Salem in 1692 and was accused of torturing girls by sticking pins into poppets. The first wife of Ann's second husband had died while Ann was caring for her, and people wondered if Ann had hastened her death to steal her husband. A Salem neighbor whose mortar and pestle Ann borrowed caught smallpox, which was taken as further proof of her guilt.

WILMOT READ: Very little documentation from Wilmot Read's trial has survived, but we do know a few details. When one of her Marblehead neighbors accused her of stealing some linens, Wilmot cursed at her and said she would not be able to urinate or defecate. The woman did have severe bowel and urinary problems for many months until she moved away from Marblehead. Wilmot also liked to tell neighbors she hated that a bloody cleaver would be found in their children's cribs. People in Marblehead reported seeing a phantom cleaver hovering over their children's beds before they became ill.

MARGARET SCOTT: A Rowley widow, Margaret Scott was accused of sending her specter to knock over her neighbor Mary Daniel's chair while Mary was sitting in it. This caused her such a great shock that she had seizures and fits, during which she saw Margaret Scott and other witches torturing her. She was also accused of harming other neighbors, including a Captain Wycomb, who claimed that, while invisible, she had beaten him with a stick.

SAMUEL WARDWELL: In addition to being a farmer and woodworker, Andover's Samuel Wardwell worked as a fortuneteller. Even worse than telling fortunes was telling them accurately, and many of Wardwell's predictions did come true—a sure sign of trafficking with Satan to the Puritan ministers. Wardwell confessed to signing a book brought to him by a man who claimed he was a Prince of the Air. This man, who was accompanied by many cats and was clearly the devil, promised Wardwell fame and fortune. Wardwell also confessed that Mary Taylor and Jane Lilly of Reading had signed the book but later recanted and admitted he lied. The magistrates did not believe him and sentenced him to death.

SARAH WILDES: Sarah Wildes of Topsfield had led a scandalous life. She had once been publicly whipped for fornication, wore expensive clothes and married her husband only seven months after his first wife died. One of her stepchildren had earlier accused her of being a witch, and neighbors accused her of sending a strange canine creature to scare their oxen into a creek. The hay fell from a wagon the oxen were pulling and was ruined. Other neighbors claimed she had made their animals sicken and die. Gossip and innuendo were enough to convince the magistrates of her guilt.

JOHN WILLARD: A young farmer who lived in Salem Village or Boxford, John Willard also served as a constable and arrested many of those accused of witchcraft. However, he soon developed doubts and denounced the trials as false. The afflicted girls in turn accused him of being a witch, and he fled town. He was captured and brought back to Salem for his trial, where the afflicted saw ghosts of people they said he murdered crowding around him in the courtroom. Although these ghosts were invisible to the magistrates, they still found Willard guilty and sentenced him to death.

# THE SALEM WITCH TRIALS: "MORE WEIGHT"

In addition to the nineteen people executed, several died in jail during the trials, including Lydia Dustin, Ann Foster, Sarah Osborne and Roger Toothaker. But eighty-year-old Giles Corey's death is perhaps the most notorious of all that occurred during the witch trials.

Salem's Howard Street Cemetery, the site of Giles Corey's death. *Photo by author.*

One reason the court was able get confessions from so many accused witches was that it used torture. Although torture was illegal under the laws of the time, the court felt its use was justified by the dire nature of the supernatural assault on the community. For example, Martha Carrier's teenage sons, Andrew and Richard, at first denied that they or their mother were witches. The court ordered them tied backward "neck to heels," a painful procedure that caused the boys to bleed from their mouths and noses. Unsurprisingly, after being tortured, they both confessed that they and their mother had pledged themselves to the devil. Torture was illegal but effective.

Giles Corey was an elderly farmer with a reputation for both stupidity and violence. When his wife, Martha, was accused of witchcraft, he sided against her, claiming he had seen her bewitch some of their animals, but the afflicted girls soon turned on Giles himself, accusing him of being a warlock. Rather than confess and save himself, as most people did, or plead innocence like his wife, Giles refused to answer any questions posed to him by the court. He simply stopped talking.

This infuriated the magistrates, who were determined to get a confession out of him. On September 19, 1692, they ordered Sheriff George Corwin to tie Giles Corey to the ground in a field across from the Salem jail. Facing up to the sky, boards were laid across his chest. When asked for a confession, Giles remained silent. As a crowd gathered, the sheriff and his men proceeded to pile stones on his chest. When asked again for a confession, Giles still said nothing. More stones, heavier and larger, were added to the pile on the old man's chest. Sheriff Corwin asked if he had anything to say. Giles Corey's only reply was: "More weight."

Those were his last words. The sheriff's men piled still more stones on top of him. The massive pile of stones crushed Giles's chest, and as he died, his tongue protruded from his mouth. Sheriff Corwin used his walking stick to push it back in.

Giles's dramatic and gruesome death inspired a folk ballad that was popular in the nineteenth century:

> *Giles Corey was a Wizard strong,*
> *A stubborn wretch was he;*
> *And fitt was he to hang on high*
> *Upon the Locust-Tree.*
>
> *So when before the magistrates*
> *For triall he did come*
> *He would no confession make,*
> *But was compleatlie dumbe…*
>
> *They got them then a heavy beam,*
> *They laid it on his breast;*
> *They loaded it with heavy stones,*
> *And hard upon him prest.*
>
> *"More weight!" now said this wretched man;*
> *"More weight!" again he cried;*
> *And he did no confession make,*
> *But wickedly he dyed.*

Giles Corey is reported to still haunt the field where he died, which is now Salem's Howard Street Cemetery. His ghost often appears before disaster strikes, most memorably in 1914 before a major fire destroyed large parts of Salem. His vengeful spirit was also said to afflict anyone who held the office of sheriff of Salem, cursing them with heart and blood ailments. George

Damage from the Salem fire of 1914. *Boston Public Library.*

Corwin died of a painful heart attack at a young age, as did many other Salem lawmen. It appears the curse was broken only when the sheriff's office was relocated to the town of Middleton.

The Salem witch trials ended almost as suddenly as they began. In the fall of 1692, the afflicted girls, emboldened with power, named the wife of Governor Phipps as a witch. Doubts had already been growing in the colony about the trials. How could there be so many witches in such a small place? Wasn't the court placing too much credence in "spectral evidence," which only the girls could see? Governor Phipps shut down the Court of Oyer and Terminer, and spectral evidence was banned from any future witchcraft trials.

The trials had ended, but much damage had been done. Salem and Salem Village were even more divided politically than before, and the reputations of the ministers and magistrates who led the trials were severely damaged. Reverend Samuel Parris, whose daughter and niece had started the trials, left Salem and returned to the Caribbean. Ann Putnam Jr., one of the afflicted girls, publicly begged the community for forgiveness, and the colony's clergy declared an Official Day of Humiliation in January 1697.

## SALEM WITCHCRAFT IN THE NINETEENTH CENTURY

Although the people of Salem were done with witchcraft, it appears that witchcraft was not done with them. A minor witch craze happened in 1811, when a poor woman named Miss Bancroft moved from Boston to Salem's Windmill Point. Miss Bancroft, who might have been a former prostitute, began to have fits and utter prophecies shortly after arriving. The fits, she said, were caused by a woman in Boston who had bewitched her. A minister tending to her convulsions agreed, saying he could see an invisible spirit tormenting her.

Although there was doubt about the legitimacy of her affliction, crowds began to gather to hear her predictions. The crowds grew larger and larger, eventually swelling to more than one thousand people. Fearing a repeat of 1692's events, the city authorities suggested that Miss Bancroft leave town—or be sent to the Salem Work House. She left immediately for Maine, apparently taking the tormenting spirit with her.

The witch trials of 1692 are Salem's most famous, but in 1878, another witchcraft trial was held in Salem. Interestingly, it involves Mary Baker Eddy, the founder of the Christian Science Church.

The case had its beginning several years earlier, when Mary Baker Eddy taught the art of Christian Science healing to Daniel and Mary Spofford of Salem. She charged them $100 and also asked for 10 percent of any revenue they made as Christian Science practitioners. The Spoffords set up a successful practice on the North Shore but neglected to send any of their revenue to Mary Baker Eddy.

Christian Science, which involves healing through prayer, was quite popular at the time,

Mary Baker Eddy, founder of the Christian Science Church. *Library of Congress, Prints and Photographs Division.*

and another practitioner named Mrs. Rawson established an office in Lynn. Mrs. Rawson successfully treated many clients, including one Lucretia Brown of Ipswich. For many years, a chronic spinal condition had left Lucretia immobilized, but after being treated by Mrs. Rawson, she was able to walk again.

Unfortunately, Lucretia Brown lost her newfound mobility one day after Daniel Spofford visited her home. She suspected that Spofford had used his powers to undo Mrs. Rawson's healing, a conjecture that Mrs. Rawson confirmed. Lucretia decided to take Spofford to court to prevent him from bewitching her again. She was supported in her efforts by Mary Baker Eddy, who was of course still unhappy about not receiving commission from the Spoffords.

A *Boston Globe* article of the time notes:

> *In an interview with a sister of Miss Brown, the latter being out of town, the lady informed the* Globe *reporter that she and her family believed there was no limit to the awful power of mesmerism, but still she had some faith in the power of the law, and thought that Dr. Spofford might be awed into abstaining from injuring her sister further.*

Ultimately, Lucretia Brown (and Mary Baker Eddy) received no satisfaction from the court. The judge overseeing the case dismissed it, saying it had no legal validity. Happily, it was the last witchcraft case heard in Salem.

# PEG WESSON, THE WITCH OF GLOUCESTER

There are no court records available about Margaret "Peg" Wesson, the witch of Gloucester; instead, her story exists in that hazy area between history and myth.

According to legend, Old Peg lived in Gloucester during the 1700s in a decrepit building called the Garrison House (which apparently is no longer standing). She was somewhat eccentric, so she naturally acquired a reputation for being a witch.

In 1758, a group of young men from Gloucester was conscripted into the army for the French and Indian War. The night before the men departed for duty in Canada, they got drunk and caroused through town. In their drunken wanderings, they encountered Old Peg, whom they teased and taunted.

Furious, Old Peg cursed them: "You drunken louts! You'll feel my wrath at the Fortress of Louisburg! You'll regret the day you insulted me!'

The men laughed and wandered off. They were soldiers now—what did they have to fear from an old woman?

Several months later, the Gloucester men found themselves stationed outside the Fortress of Louisburg, the immense French stronghold that controlled the St. Lawrence River. A battle had been raging for weeks over the fortress, and as they hunkered down to avoid French gunfire, an enormous black crow appeared in the sky above them.

With a frightful croak, the ominous bird swooped down toward the Gloucester battalion, trying to claw them with its razor-sharp claws. The men shooed it away, but it swept down again and again. It was if the crow were trying to force them into the open and expose them to the French muskets.

One of the men said, "Remember the night before we left home? I bet that crow's really Old Peg." Raising his musket, he fired a bullet straight into the bird's heart, but incredibly the crow was unaffected and with a malevolent caw, it once again began its aerial assault.

The man raised his musket to take another shot, but one of his fellows pushed the gun down, saying, "You can't hurt a witch with a lead musket ball. You need silver. Watch this."

He pulled one of the silver buttons off his jacket, loaded it into his musket and fired at the crow. The silver button flew through the air and hit the bird squarely in one leg. With a horrific shriek, it fell from the sky. The men continued the battle unmolested by the crow and were eventually victorious.

When the Gloucester men returned home, they heard some strange news. The same day they had shot the crow, Old Peg had suddenly fallen and broken her leg. When the town physician came to fix the wound, he pulled something unusual out her leg. It was a silver button.

# THE GOOD WITCHES OF THE NORTH SHORE

Although most witches were feared for their malevolent powers, Edward Dimond of Marblehead and his granddaughter Moll Pitcher of Lynn were respected for their ability to help people.

Edward Dimond was a sailor by trade, but he was called Wizard Dimond or simply Old Dimond by his neighbors and was famous for his

The Old Brigg House, Edward Dimond and Moll Pitcher's home in Marblehead. *Library of Congress, Prints and Photographs Division.*

magical powers. He claimed that these powers had run in his family for many generations and that he was the descendant of famous astrologers.

On stormy nights, Wizard Dimond would make his way to a graveyard that was located on a hill overlooking the sea and give supernatural aid to ships caught in the rough weather. Stalking among the gravestones, he would magically give orders and advice to ships far out to sea. Although Marblehead was nowhere in sight, sailors at the helm would hear the voice of Wizard Dimond in their ears telling them how to steer their ships safely through the wild waves.

At other times, Wizard Dimond used his powers to punish evildoers. A story told in Marblehead claims that one cold day, a poor widow came to Dimond's house in great distress. One of her neighbors had stolen her firewood and refused to give it back. The constable didn't believer her, so she had come to plead for the wizard's help. After hearing her story, he agreed to use his magical powers to bring about justice.

That night, the thief woke suddenly from a deep sleep and found himself controlled by a strange compulsion. Walking to the pile of stolen wood, he took the heaviest log he could find and laid it across his back. Against his will, he walked out of his house and through the town carrying the log. He walked back and forth without rest until sunrise, when he collapsed on the ground with exhaustion and cried out for forgiveness. Wizard Dimond's spell had worked. The widow got her wood back, and the thief never stole again.

Edward's granddaughter Mary was born in Marblehead in 1738 but moved to Lynn with her husband, a cobbler named Robert Pitcher. He was not very successful at his trade, so Mary, known by her nickname Moll, decided to carry on her family's tradition and became a fortuneteller. It was something she was quite skilled at, and her reputation spread. Sailors and merchants who wanted advice on when to sail formed the largest part of her clientele.

Lynn historian James Robinson Newhall described her business best:

> *There was no port on either continent where floated the flag of an American ship that had not heard of the fame of Moll Pitcher. To her came the rich and poor, the wise and ignorant, the accomplished and the vulgar, the timid and the brave. The ignorant sailor who believed in omens and dreams of superstition, and the intelligent merchant whose ships were freighted for distant lands alike sought her dwelling, and many a vessel has been deserted by its crew and waited idly at the wharves for weeks in consequence of her unlucky predictions. Many persons came from places far remote to consult her about affairs of the heart—love, loss of property or vicissitudes of the future being found to be some of her most faithful predictions.*

Moll lived in and ran her business from a small, unassuming cottage at the foot of Lynn's High Rock. The house stood on the north side of what is now Essex Street. The neighborhood at that time was somewhat desolate, and small children were afraid to walk near her house after dark. But adults weren't afraid of the prophetess, and clients who came looking for Moll's house knew they were close when they saw an unusual landmark. Her neighbor across the street, a Dr. Henry Burchstead, had a gateway made of two whale ribs. In lieu of a sign, these served as a marker guiding people to Moll's house. (Dr. Burchstead had acquired the ribs from a beached whale so large he reportedly rode into its mouth on horseback.)

When clients arrived at Moll's house, her daughter Becky seated them in the front room. Becky would tell them her mother was out at the moment but would be right back and then would engage them in conversation.

Moll Pitcher's gravestone in Lynn. *Photo by author.*

Often, Moll was really in the next room secretly listening to what the clients told Becky. When she finally entered the front room, the visitors would be amazed by her incredible foreknowledge of their situation.

Moll's preferred method of fortunetelling was to read tea leaves. After making a cup of tea, she would pour out the liquid and then turn out the tea leaves onto a saucer. The arrangement of the leaves helped her decide the client's future. For example, if the leaves formed a long line, it meant he would live a long life and leave behind many grandchildren. If the leaves were scattered all over the saucer, it meant he would be unlucky in love, but if the leaves were in a group, it indicated romantic success. Moll's success as a fortuneteller suggests there was more to her method than just reading tea leaves, but sadly, there are no surviving records of any of her sessions.

Moll died in 1813, leaving behind a son and three daughters, including Becky. For many years, her grave in Lynn's Western Burial Ground was unmarked, but the city erected a monument on it in 1887.

Moll's reputation grew after her death. The poet John Greenleaf Whittier wrote a poem (which was unflattering) about her, and playwright John Jones wrote a play called *Moll Pitcher; or the Fortune Teller of Lynn*. She was also credited with helping the Americans defeat the British during the Revolution. For example, an article in a 1938 issue of the *Boston Globe* claims she warned the Sons of Liberty that the British were marching on Lexington, located buried pirate gold to finance the American army and foretold George Washington's ultimate triumph in the war. The same article also claims that Moll Pitcher predicted the invention of the submarine and the radio and that, in the future, only the poor would live in Boston while the rich lived in "houses like palaces" outside it.

I would take these claims about Moll's involvement with the Revolution or her historic predictions with a very big grain of salt. The idea that she helped the American army against the British seems to come originally from an 1895 novel by Mary Ellen Griffin Hoey called *Moll Pitcher's Prophecies, or The American Sibyl*. There also seems to be some confusion between Moll Pitcher, the fortuneteller from Lynn, and Molly Pitcher, a semi-legendary figure who brought water to American soldiers during the Revolution.

Moll Pitcher didn't write down any prophecies, so I'm not sure from where the predictions about technological inventions or Boston's future came. They aren't from Moll, and given the number of luxury condos being built in Boston, they don't appear accurate.

*Chapter 3*
# PIRATES AND BURIED TREASURE

While the North Shore's communities were divided internally by witchcraft claims, a more tangible menace threatened them at sea: pirates. But although pirates were lawless and murderous, rumors also claimed their treasure was buried in various secret locations along the coast. Stolen gold and jewels could be unearthed if someone were clever enough—and brave enough to face the supernatural creatures that guarded them.

## JOHN QUELCH, THE ACCIDENTAL PIRATE

John Quelch was hanged in Boston on June 30, 1704, for the crime of piracy. Pleading innocent until the very end, Quelch claimed he was just the victim of a misunderstanding. The Boston court didn't believe him, but I suggest you read on and make the decision for yourself.

Quelch's accidental descent into piracy began on July 13 of the previous year. England and its colonies were at war during this time with France, and Massachusetts's governor, Joseph Dudley, commissioned the *Charles*, an eighty-eight-ton vessel, to harass and attack French ships that traveled the waters off New England. The five wealthy Bostonians who owned the ship eagerly accepted the commission. Not only could they help England, but they could also get rich from French plunder.

Unfortunately, things didn't turn out quite the way they and Governor Dudley hoped. In late July, the *Charles* was anchored in Marblehead Harbor with a full and eager crew, but its captain, one Daniel Plowman, was too ill to set sail. From his sickbed onboard the *Charles*, Plowman sent word to Boston that he was ill and didn't feel like his crew was trustworthy. Marblehead at the time had a reputation for lawlessness and was the perfect place for the governor to recruit a band of privateers. There is a fine line between government-sanctioned privateer and lawless pirate, however, and Plowman was afraid his unruly crew might cross over it.

The ship's owners decided to find another captain for the ship, but their decision came too late. Shortly before a new captain was to be sent to Marblehead, the crew locked Captain Plowman in his cabin and set sail for the open seas. The men then appointed John Quelch as their new captain. As the *Charles* sailed out into the Atlantic, Captain Plowman's body was thrown overboard.

This sounds like mutiny, and certainly when Quelch was later brought to trial, the court viewed it that way. In his defense, Quelch claimed that despite

A replica antique sailing ship in Salem's harbor, date unknown. *Boston Public Library.*

the court's suspicions, he and his crew had not actually harmed Captain Plowman. No, Quelch said, Daniel Plowman was already dead when they threw him overboard. The crew was simply trying to accomplish the mission with which the *Charles* had been charged: attacking French ships. They were just eager to get started!

Quelch commanded that the ship sail to South America. Prowling the waters off Brazil, Quelch attacked merchant ships, military ships and even fishing boats, stealing their cargo and murdering their crews.

The hold of the *Charles* was soon filled with luxury goods and gold, but there was one major problem: Brazil was a Portuguese colony, and all the vessels Quelch attacked were Portuguese. Quelch was in violation of Governor Dudley's orders, and to compound the problem, England and Portugal had joined together in an alliance shortly after the *Charles* left Marblehead Harbor. Not only was Quelch ignoring orders, but he was also attacking one of his country's key allies.

After nine months of terrorizing Brazilian waters, the *Charles* returned to Marblehead Harbor. Its crew staggered ashore, their pockets heavy with Portuguese gold, and the town's taverns, inns and houses of ill-repute threw open their doors in welcome. Word of the gluttonous and debaucherous pirates reached Boston, and Governor Dudley sent a welcome committee of armed troops.

Quelch and many of his men were captured quite easily and seemed surprised when they were arrested. This seems to indicate that they didn't think they had broken any laws but only had been following orders. They argued to the soldiers that it was all a misunderstanding. Their pleas didn't reach sympathetic ears. Already, the captain of another North Shore ship, the *Larramore*, had decided to become a pirate after hearing about Quelch's success. The governor was determined to restore order by whatever means possible.

Twenty-five of the *Charles*'s forty-three crew members were arrested and taken to Boston for trial. The remaining eighteen escaped Governor Dudley's dragnet and fled New England. During the trial, which was presided over by Governor Dudley himself, many of the men pleaded guilty to spare their lives, and several even testified against their shipmates. In the end, only Quelch and five other men were found guilty and sentenced to be hanged.

On June 30, 1704, the doomed prisoners were led from their jail to a gallows on the banks of the Charles River near Copp's Hill in Boston's North End. The procession was headed by a man carrying a silver oar, a symbol of the authority of the British navy.

As Quelch stood on the gallows, he once again pleaded his innocence, saying:

> *Gentlemen, 'Tis but little I have to speak; what I have to say is this, I desire to be informed for what I have done. I am Condemned only upon Circumstances. I forgive all the World, so the Lord be merciful to my Soul… They should also take care how they bring money into New England, to be hanged for it.*

After hearing this final statement, the hangman brought a swift end to John Quelch's life and his accidental career as a pirate. The bodies of the executed men were taken to an island in Boston Harbor and hung up in chains as a warning to anyone else considering a similar career.

## John Phillips, the Pirate Who Was Pickled

Andrew Haraden didn't suspect what was in store for him on the morning of April 14, 1724, as he set sail from Annisquam Harbor. Haraden was the captain of a newly constructed fishing sloop called the *Squirrel*, and his thoughts were focused on the weather and on codfish, not on pirates.

After the *Squirrel* left Ipswich Bay, it was approached by another, somewhat run-down-looking ship called the *Revenge*. The waters off the North Shore were filled with ships in those days, and Captain Haraden paid little mind to the *Revenge*, even as it drew closer and closer to the *Squirrel*. It was only when the *Revenge* raised a black flag emblazoned with a skeleton that Haraden realized he was about to be attacked by pirates.

The pirates threw grappling lines onto the *Squirrel* and boarded, and Haraden told his men to surrender. They were too heavily outnumbered to put up a fight. The pirates decided that the *Squirrel* was better than their own ship and decided to make it their own. In fact, the deck of the *Squirrel* was so new that it hadn't even been finished. Haraden was commanded to stay on the ship and join the pirates; the rest of his men were put on the *Revenge* and sailed back home.

Haraden learned the captain of the pirates was John Phillips. Many years before, Phillips had been serving as the carpenter on a ship sailing from England to Newfoundland. The ship was captured by a pirate named Captain Anstis, and Phillips signed on with him. Over time, John Phillips became captain of his own crew of pirates and marauded along the North American coast and the Caribbean.

Haraden also learned that, like him, most of the men serving under Phillips had been forced into it. In fact, other than Captain Phillips, only a man named John Nutt and a handful of others had joined willingly. The rest of the pirate crew wanted to return to a lawful life, but their fear of Phillips and of Nutt, who was large and brutish, kept them obedient.

Andrew Haraden was not intimidated. After only two days at sea, he gathered around him a circle of brave men who were willing to risk their lives for freedom. Among them were John Fillmore of Ipswich and Edward Cheesman. Cheesman was large and muscular, and Haraden thought he would be able to overpower Nutt. Cheesman was also the ship's carpenter, and they decided to use his tools to fight the pirates.

The mutiny took place on April 17. To begin their plan, Cheesman placed his tools around the deck. Various other men who were also part of the mutiny took their places as if they were finishing the deck. Then they waited for the signal to attack.

Cheesman approached John Nutt and offered to show him the work being done on the deck. As they walked, they passed Haraden, who winked at Cheesman. This was the signal he had been waiting on. Cheesman abruptly reached between Nutt's legs and squeezed as hard as he could. Nutt gasped, and Cheesman grabbed his collar with his other hand. Cheesman then threw Nutt over the side of the ship.

Nutt clung to the ship's rail with one hand and pleaded for his life, but Cheesman pounded on Nutt's hand. With a cry, the pirate fell into the ocean and drowned.

When John Fillmore saw Cheesman attack Nutt, he picked up the axe he had been working with and swung it at the boatswain, another pirate loyal to Captain Phillips. The blow reportedly cleft the boatswain's head cleanly down the middle.

Hearing the commotion, Captain Phillips came on deck from his cabin. Cheesman struck him hard with a mallet, but it only stunned the pirate. Phillips quickly recovered from the blow and rushed toward Cheesman. Haraden grabbed another axe and killed the pirate instantly with a blow to the head.

During the fighting, several other pirates were killed, and four surviving pirates who had willingly served Phillips were bound with rope as prisoners. Captain Phillips's head was nailed to the mast as a gruesome war trophy. Haraden took command of the *Squirrel* again and set sail for Annisquam.

Many of the pirates were sent to Boston for trial, and Phillips's head was sent along in a pickle barrel as evidence. In the end, only two were convicted, including a man named John Rose Archer, who had also served under the notorious Blackbeard. The other pirates had all helped Haraden in one way or another and were set free.

The two men were hanged in Boston on June 2, 1724. When Archer climbed onto the gallows, he gave a speech repenting his crimes and said, "But one Wickedness that has led me as much as any, to all the rest, has been my brutish Drunkenness. By strong Drink I have been heated and hardened into the Crimes that are now more bitter than Death unto me."

Because he had such a long career in piracy, Archer's body was hung in an iron gibbet in Boston Harbor as a warning to others. The records do not indicate what happened to Captain Phillips's pickled head.

## FANNY CAMPBELL SAVES THE DAY

Here's a story that seems too amazing to be true, but according to multiple sources, the following events really did happen.

The story begins in Lynn in the year 1773. Two fisherman, Henry Campbell and Richard Lovell, lived next to each other at the foot High Rock. Richard Lovell had a nineteen-year-old son named William, who was adept at sailing and was eager to make his living on the high seas. Although he dreamt of being a sea captain, he planned to always return to Lynn because he was in love with Henry Campbell's eighteen-year-old daughter, Fanny.

Fanny's spirit of adventure was an equal match for William's. While most women in Lynn spent their days working inside the home or farming, Fanny spent hers fishing in her father's boat, hunting in the woods outside Lynn and riding horses until late at night. When William announced that he was planning to join the crew of the *Royal Kent*, a vessel bound for the West Indies from Boston, Fanny gave him her blessing. She had no desire to prevent William from following his dream. As they parted, William promised Fanny that he would remember her and come back to Lynn, no matter what befell him.

The *Royal Kent* had an uneventful voyage down to the West Indies, but as it neared Haiti, a ship flying the skull and crossbones appeared and pursued the merchant vessel. The *Royal Kent* was a well-armed ship, and the captain ordered the cannons to be fired at the encroaching pirate ship. Heavy damage was done to the marauder, but not enough to stop its crew from boarding the *Royal Kent*. Fierce fighting ensued. The captain of the *Royal Kent* and the pirate captain both died in the bloody mêlée, but the pirates ultimately won the battle. They scuttled the *Royal Kent* and conscripted its remaining crew, including William Lovell, into their pirate band.

Meanwhile, Fanny Campbell waited patiently for William to return to her. A new suitor had appeared at her door almost as soon as William left for Boston. His name was Robert Burnet, and he was a captain in the British navy. Although he was young, handsome and charming, Fanny resisted his advances. She knew that someday William would come back to Lynn. Besides, revolution was brewing at this time in the English colonies. Captain Burnet was a staunch supporter of the English king, while Fanny felt the colonists should have the right of self-government.

As Fanny firmly but politely rebuffed the captain's advances, William plotted his escape from the pirate ship. One night, when the ship was off the coast of Cuba, William and two friends, Jack Herbert and Henry Breed, lowered a small boat and made for the island. But rather than finding freedom in Cuba, they found themselves in an even worse situation. Upon arriving in Cuba, they were charged with piracy and thrown into prison.

Months went by. In Lynn, William Lovell's family gave up hope of his return and assumed he was dead, but Fanny continued to wait faithfully. Captain Burnet continued to visit and plead his love but was always rebuffed.

Two years after William set sail for the West Indies, a haggard sailor arrived in Lynn bearing letters for the Lovell family and Fanny Campbell. It was William's friend Jack Herbert, who had escaped from Havana and made his way back to Massachusetts on an American vessel.

Fanny rejoiced to hear that William was still alive and closely questioned Jack Herbert about the prison where he was imprisoned. Where was it located? How high were the walls? How heavily was it guarded? After Jack told her everything he knew, she said, "In a few days, a man named Mr. Channing will come visit you. He will have a plan to free William. Promise me you'll follow his directions!"

Jack promised, and a few days later, a young sailor named Channing came to Jack Herbert's house in Boston's North End. A ship called the *Constance* was sailing for Cuba the next day, and Channing had signed up himself and Jack as crew. When they arrived in Havana, they would free William. Jack agreed to Channing's plan, and the next morning, the *Constance* left Boston Harbor with the two young sailors on board.

Channing was a skilled sailor, and the captain, an Englishman named Brownless, appointed him second mate. The voyage south went smoothly, but one night, as Channing was walking below decks, he overheard Brownless and the first mate, another Englishman named Banning, talking quietly in the captain's cabin. There had been a change in plans, the captain said. Yes, they were still going to Cuba, but after leaving Havana, they would head straight for England. War with the colonies was coming, and the king's navy needed seamen. The American crew of the *Constance* would be conscripted into the Royal Navy. Not for long, though—only three years.

Three years! Channing stood in shock outside the captain's cabin. Their chances of returning to Lynn with William Lovell seemed slim. Something needed to be done.

The next day, Channing, armed with two pistols and a sword, barged into Brownless's cabin. He declared himself captain and tied up the English captain. The crew, who were almost all American born, threw their support behind Channing when they learned about Captain Brownless's plan. Brownless admitted defeat and agreed to support Channing.

Channing's position as captain did not go unchallenged, however. The ship's first mate, Banning, and the ship's cook plotted to kill Channing while he slept. The cook, armed with the galley's sharpest knife, crept silently below decks toward Channing's cabin. It was pitch dark, and he walked with his hand outstretched in front of him. Suddenly, as he reached Channing's door, he felt a man in front of him. He stabbed forward with all his strength, but as his knife struck flesh, he felt a blade pierce his own side. With a scream, he toppled onto the floor. Another body landed on top of him with a heavy thud.

The crew came running with lanterns, and Channing opened the door to his cabin. One the floor lay the cook, dying from his wound, and Captain Brownless. Banning and the cook had not included Brownless in their plan, and he had developed the same plan on his own. Brownless and the cook had killed each other, each mistakenly assuming in the darkness that the other was Channing.

After capturing the *George*, a British ship, the *Constance* finally reached Havana. Jack Herbert and eight other men set out for the prison. Jack knew that the guards patrolled the prison in four pairs, so the American pirates waited patiently in the darkness, overpowering each pair of Cuban guards as they walked by. After freeing William Lovell and Henry Breed from their cell, the men made their way back to the *George*. Both ships raised anchor and set sail for Massachusetts.

On board the *Constance*, William Lovell was brought below decks to Captain Channing's cabin. Locking the door, Channing threw his arms around William and kissed him passionately. William jumped back in surprise, but as he looked closely at Channing, he realized the young captain was really his beloved Fanny Campbell. Fanny explained that she had dressed as a man to free him, but none of the other crew suspected she was a woman. If they found out their captain was female, there would be mutiny. William agreed to keep her secret.

On the return trip to New England, the *Constance* and the *George* encountered another British merchant ship. While plundering its cargo, they learned from the crew that England and its American colonies were now officially at war. No longer were Fanny and her crew lawless pirates; they declared themselves privateers who would prey on the colonists' enemies.

When the two ships under Fanny's command were two days out from Boston, they met a British warship, the *Dolphin*. Fighting broke out between the privateers and the *Dolphin*, but Fanny's men eventually boarded the warship and subdued its crew. When the *Dolphin*'s captain

The cover of Maturin Murray Ballou's 1844 book about Fanny Campbell. *Library of Congress, Prints and Photographs Division.*

was brought to "Captain Channing's" cabin for questioning, Fanny couldn't hide her amazement. The enemy captain was Robert Burnet, the young British naval officer who had wooed her in Lynn.

As she had done with William, Fanny revealed her true identity and swore Captain Burnet to secrecy. Because he loved her, he agreed to keep her secret, although revealing her identity would have created dissent among the crew and perhaps helped him get free.

The next day, the *Constance* and the *George* arrived in Marblehead, and Fanny and William returned to Lynn. They were married shortly thereafter and raised several children. William continued to serve as a privateer during the Revolutionary War, while Fanny taught their sons and daughters to hunt, fish and, of course, sail.

# BURIED TREASURE IN BYFIELD?

With so many pirates active off the shore, it's not surprising that Massachusetts has treasure buried in its soil. But the pirate treasure buried in Byfield, a village in Newbury, wasn't buried by a pirate at all.

To clarify, the treasure did originally belong to a notorious pirate: Roger Hayman. Hayman was a successful pirate who preyed on British and American ships in the late 1700s, but in February 1800, his luck ran out. The British and American navies, so often bitter enemies, combined forces to defeat their common foe.

The battle took place off the coast of Haiti. Heavy casualties were suffered on both sides, and Hayman himself was severely wounded. With his pirate fleet destroyed, he fled back to his home country of England on the remaining ship. He brought with him two chests of gold coins, which had been taken from a British warship during the sea battle. Intended as payment for the sailors, the coins were now Hayman's personal treasure.

Hayman planned to have his family in Liverpool tend to his wounds, but when he arrived home, he received disturbing news. His wife and children had immigrated to New York to start a new life and left instructions for Hayman to follow them. Despite his injuries, Hayman booked passage on a ship to America, bringing the chests of gold with him.

Hayman didn't tell anyone onboard his true identity or reveal what was in his chests, but two of his fellow passengers, a businessman named Stearns Compton and a physician known only as Dr. Griffin, recognized Hayman and guessed what was in his luggage. They kept a close watch on the wounded pirate during the voyage.

The difficult crossing was more than Roger Hayman's grievously injured body could withstand. He died before the ship reached its first stop, which was Newburyport, Massachusetts. While the ship unloaded its cargo and refreshed supplies before departing for New York, Dr. Griffin and Stearns Compton absconded with the dead pirate's golden treasure. After scouting out a good location, Griffin and Compton secretly removed the coins from the ship and loaded them onto a hired oxcart. They then buried the treasure at the chosen spot, which was a distinctive rock on a small, marshy island near the farming community of Byfield. The rock was a large boulder balanced on a smaller one, but to make double sure they would recognize it when they returned, they also carved the letter "A" onto it. After their work was done, they returned to the ship and sailed to New York City, vowing that they would return to Byfield for the treasure in five years, once the memory of Roger Hayman and his stolen gold had been forgotten.

As so often happens in these tales of piracy, their plans did not work out as they expected. Griffin and Compton were unaware that a small Byfield boy named Howard Noyes had witnessed the burial. Young Howard had been sitting in a tree when the two conspirators arrived and had remained hidden in the foliage as they hid the treasure. After Griffin and Compton departed, he raced home to his family's farm, where he told his parents that he knew where pirate treasure had been buried. His parents, being practical and unimaginative New England farmers, punished him for making up stories.

Despite being punished, Howard continued telling people that pirate treasure was buried in the marsh. Word spread throughout the village and beyond, and soon the distinctive balancing rock with the "A" carved on it was besieged by people digging for gold. Because the area was quite marshy, and because Griffin and Compton had hidden the exact burial spot under leaves and branches, no one succeeded at finding the treasure. Griffin and Compton were never able to return and retrieve the stolen coins because of the crowds and publicity.

In the 1930s, a local laborer was rumored to have paid for things with gold coins that had been minted in the 1700s. Had he found Roger Hayman's treasure? The laborer left town soon afterward, and the story has never been confirmed. For the curious, the balanced rock inscribed with the "A" still sits on Kent Island near the Parker River, bearing mute witness to the location of the pirate's gold.

## HARRY MAIN AND THE TREASURE CATS

New England's folklore is full of stories about people who find buried treasure only to discover it is watched over by a supernatural guardian. As this next story illustrates, finding a pirate's golden hoard doesn't necessarily mean you get to keep it.

The pirate in this case was a man named Harry Main, who lived in Ipswich during its earliest years. Piracy was only one of Harry's many crimes. He was also a robber, a murderer and, worst of all to his pious Puritan neighbors, a blasphemer.

Late in his life, Harry embarked on new a career as a ship wrecker. On dark, stormy nights, Harry would sneak down to the sandbars off the coast

An antique postcard depicting the Ipswich dunes. *Boston Public Library.*

of Ipswich and light beacon lanterns. Out at sea, sailors would see Harry's lights. Thinking they showed the safe channel into Ipswich Harbor, the sailors wrecked their vessels on the sandbars and drowned in the rough surf. Harry kept any gold that he found in the wreckage and sold any cargo that could be salvaged.

When the citizens of Ipswich learned about Harry's newest business venture, they executed him for his murderous crimes. They could only serve human justice, but divine justice was served in the form of a curse. After his death, Harry was doomed to haunt the sandbars and beaches of Ipswich and make chains from sand for eternity. Ipswich legend says that Harry's screams of rage and frustration can still be heard on stormy nights, when the chains he has made are blown away by the howling winds.

People living on Plum Island remained indoors during storms for fear that they would encounter his malevolent specter, and people all along the coast said that his howls would predict when a storm was about to hit. Harry's ghost also haunted a neighbor's house on Water Street until the local ministers all joined forces in prayer and expelled him.

After his death, Harry's neighbors ransacked his house and dug up his garden in an attempt to find his gold, but their searches were futile. Wherever his gold was hidden, it wasn't on his property. A house that was said to be

Harry Main's house supposedly stood near this empty lot in Ipswich. It is private property, so please don't dig for treasure! *Photo by author.*

Harry Main's stood in Ipswich until the middle of the twentieth century, when it was finally torn down.

A few years after Harry's demise, an Ipswich man started to dream about the buried treasure. For three nights in a row, he dreamt he was digging on a certain hill outside town. Realizing these were not dreams but prophetic visions, the next evening, the man set out under the cover of darkness with a shovel to find the gold.

In addition to the shovel, he carried his Bible. The man knew that a blaspheming pirate like Harry had probably cursed the treasure, and he hoped the Bible would protect him from malevolent magic. The man also resolved to remain totally silent as he dug for the treasure. The wise old folks in Ipswich said that a person could resist any enchantment by remaining silent. But they warned that even speaking a single word would open someone up to the power of a witch or warlock.

The man came to the hill he had seen in his dreams and began to dig. He dug for many hours until the full moon was directly above him, shining down into the deep pit in which he stood. Suddenly, his shovel struck something solid.

After using his hands to clear the dirt, the man saw a heavy stone slab with a large iron bar next to it. He suspected that Harry had hidden his treasure under the stone and left the iron bar nearby so it could be lifted. The man stuck the iron bar under the slab. The treasure was almost within his reach!

But as he began to pry up the heavy stone, he felt something rub against his leg. He jumped back in surprise and saw that it was a black cat. Another cat appeared in the pit and then another. As the three cats howled and hissed at the man, even more felines appeared in the pit.

The man began to panic. The pit was now full of cats, all of them baring their teeth and swiping at him with their claws. As he looked up, he saw cats patrolling the rim of the pit, their eyes luminous in the moonlight. He was trapped.

"Scat!" he blurted out. "Get away from me!" As soon as those words left his mouth, the man regretted saying them. He had broken the rule of magical silence.

In a flash, the cats disappeared, and as the man watched in horror, the pit began to fill with icy water. He grabbed the iron bar, but the water quickly rose up to his neck, and he had to climb out of the pit before he could pry up the stone slab. As soon as he reached the surface, the pit collapsed on itself. The man had escaped with his life but without the treasure. Realizing that Harry Main's gold was cursed, he resolved to let it remain buried. He walked back into town carrying the iron bar, which was made into the latch for his front door. For many years, the iron bar was pointed out to visitors as proof of his story.

The story of Harry Main and his guardian cats seems too fantastic to be true, but Thomas Franklin Waters notes in his 1905 book, *Ipswich in the Massachusetts Bay Colony*, that a fisherman named Henry Maine did indeed live in Ipswich in the 1670s and was probably the Harry Main on whom the legend was based. Does his soul still wander the beaches and sandbars near Ipswich? I don't know, and I'm not going to spend a dark, stormy night out there finding out.

# The Treasure of Pine Point

Another story about buried treasure is found in James Robinson Newhall's 1880 book, *Lin: Or Jewels of the Third Plantation*. According to Newhall, back in the late 1600s, the Old Anchor Tavern in Lynn was a popular spot for people traveling between Boston and Salem. It was a hotspot for news and gossip, and several men who were regulars at the tavern heard an interesting rumor. According to the rumor, a pirate had buried his treasure underneath a tree at Pine Point near the mouth of the Saugus River. The pirate had vanished long ago and was believed to be dead, but his treasure had never been located.

The men from the tavern set out one moonlit night to try their luck at finding the gold. To help them, they brought along a local Indian man named David Kunkshamooshaw. Kunkshamooshaw was the grandson of Winnepurkit, the great sachem who was mentioned in the first chapter of this book. Kunkshamooshaw lived in small house underneath a large cedar tree called the Indian Tree. Although the Pennacooks' political power had long been broken, Kunkshamooshaw was admired in Lynn for his magical skills. He was known to be a powerful powwow.

When the men arrived at Pine Point, Kunkshamooshaw used a forked branch of hazel wood as a dowsing rod. He walked slowly around the tree where the pirate had buried his treasure. As he walked, the branch constantly vibrated in his hands, but when he reached a certain spot, the branch pointed abruptly pointed downward.

"This is where the treasure is buried," the shaman said. "But before we begin digging, I will draw a protective circle on the ground. This will keep out any spirits that try to stop us. But be warned! Whatever happens, don't say a single word. All our work will be undone if you do."

Kunkshamooshaw muttered magic incantations and drew a large circle around the tree with the hazel branch. When he was done, he and the other men stepped inside and began to dig. At first, they struck nothing but sand, but after only a short while, they hit a large slab of rock.

As soon as they did, a heavy wind picked up. Although they were buffeted by wind and blinded by the sand, the men kept digging. Once the slab of stone was fully clear, they pulled a large branch from the tree and began to pry up the stone. Soon, the treasure would be theirs!

When they lifted the slab, they glimpsed a large ironbound chest, but as they did, they heard the sound of thundering hooves galloping toward them. From the darkness, an enormous horse appeared, bearing on its bare back a gigantic man with long, wild hair. It was the pirate's ghost.

The men dropped their tools in panic, but although the undead rider and his steed charged repeatedly at the treasure seekers, the magic circle always repelled them. Through his monstrous grin, the pirate shouted angrily, "By my blood, what do ye here? Ye are well set to work filching my gold, hard earned upon the sea by dagger and by fire. But the devil will yet save his own, I wot. Aroynt ye, or bear a pirate's malediction!"

With that, the horse reared high up on its rear legs, its sharp hooves poised to strike down on Kunkshamooshaw's head. Unable to control himself, the shaman cried out in fear. The magic circle's power was broken. The horse's hooves struck downward, narrowly missing the shaman and slamming the stone slab back into place. The shaman and the other men fled terrified into the woods, while the pirate and his horse rode off over the ocean waves into the darkness. The pirate's malevolent laughter echoed after the men as they ran all the way back to the Old Anchor.

No one from Lynn ever tried to find the pirate's treasure again, and I suppose it must still be buried somewhere in the sand. Pine Point is now a nice residential neighborhood, so don't go digging in anyone's backyard! Sadly, the cedar tree that stood by David Kunkshamooshaw's house was chopped down many years ago, and the land where he lived was flooded to make one of the city's reservoirs.

## THOMAS VEAL AND THE TREASURE OF PIRATE'S GLEN

In 1658, a great earthquake hit New England. Not only did it damage many towns, but it also buried one of New England's most famous pirate treasures.

Several years before the great quake, an unfamiliar ship was seen off the coast of Lynn. The people of Lynn watched suspiciously as four men came ashore from the ship in a small boat and then walked into the dense forests surrounding the Saugus River. Clearly, people said, these were pirates.

A few days later, one of the blacksmiths at the Saugus ironworks found an anonymous note on the ironworks' door. The note's writer requested that the blacksmith make some handcuffs, leg manacles and hatchets and then leave them in the forest at a certain spot. The blacksmith would find silver coins left there for payment. Clearly, the blacksmith thought, this note has come from the pirates. Still, he forged the handcuffs and manacles and left them under the designated tree. As promised, silver coins had been left there as payment.

Shortly after this, the pirates were seen sailing away from Lynn, but they returned the following year with a new companion: a beautiful young woman. Once again, the pirates took a small boat up the Saugus River and traipsed into the woods, but this time they built a small house in a glen now known as Pirate's Glen. They also planted a garden and dug a well. It appeared to the people of Lynn that the pirates had given up their thieving ways and were now, with the aid of their female friend, pursuing a more domestic way of life.

Unfortunately, their domestic bliss was quite brief. The young woman grew ill and died, and the British navy arrived in Lynn looking for the four pirates. Three of them were captured and brought back to England, where they were hanged for their crimes. The fourth, Thomas Veal, hid in a cave and avoided capture.

Rather than return to his house, Veal took up permanent residence in the cave where he had hidden and became a cobbler. Although the people of Lynn bought shoes from the former pirate, they always suspected that Veal's cave also contained pirate treasure. This was a suspicion they were never able to confirm because, in 1658, the great earthquake struck. Veal and his possessions were sealed inside the cave by tons of rock and never seen again. The buried cave has since that time been called the Pirate's Dungeon or just simply Dungeon Rock.

*Chapter 4*

# STRANGE PLACES AND WEIRD LOCATIONS

The North Shore is famous for its quaint towns, picturesque shoreline and historic homes. But not every place in the area is quite so wholesome. If you know where to look, you can also find some very strange places, including the devil's stomping grounds, a cemetery for an abandoned insane asylum and a ghost town once inhabited by witches. Be careful about what you look for. If you succeed in finding the vanishing farm of Witches Woods, you might never get home again.

## DUNGEON ROCK

As I mentioned at the end of the last chapter, the pirate Thomas Veal and his treasure were supposedly buried under tons of stone when an earthquake struck in 1658, and the stony hill he's buried under is now called Dungeon Rock. It's now the site of one of the strangest man-made structures in all of New England.

After the earthquake, people occasionally tried to find the treasure, but they were always discouraged by the enormous scope of the project. No one except Thomas Veal was certain whether there even was any treasure, and since he was dead, he wasn't available for comment. But in 1852, Thomas Veal reached out from the land of the dead and told a man named Hiram Marble to start digging

Marble was a Spiritualist. Spiritualism was started in upstate New York in 1848 by sisters Kate and Margaret Fox, and the religion claims that the spirits of the dead can communicate with the living to give advice and inspiration. Certain people, called mediums, are more attuned to the spirit world and can communicate easily with the departed. For those of us not so gifted, the spirits are more likely to manifest as rapping sounds or movements on a Ouija board.

According to Marble, Thomas Veal's spirit had said it wanted him to dig into Dungeon Rock and find the treasure. So Hiram Marble moved to Lynn, purchased the land on which Dungeon Rock stood and began digging into solid stone. Progress was incredibly slow, but Hiram persevered, even though he barely carved out one foot of tunnel per month.

I think most people would have given up after a few months, but the spirit of Thomas Veal kept promising Marble that he was drawing close to the cave where Veal's skeleton and the treasure were buried. Whenever Hiram got discouraged, he would ask a medium to consult Veal for advice.

While the medium waited outside, Hiram would write his question for the dead pirate on a piece of paper and then cover it with fifteen additional sheets of paper. When the medium entered the room, she would lay her hand on the top sheet of paper and, just by touch alone, determine what the question was. She would then write down Thomas Veal's answer. Some answers also came from Captain Harris, who supposedly had been the leader of Veal's pirate crew. Despite the histories that indicated only Veal had been buried alive, the medium claimed that Captain Harris had been buried as well.

An 1884 edition of the *Bay State Monthly* documented an example of this process. Hiram asked the pirate in what direction he should dig. The medium wrote down the following response, which she claimed came from Thomas Veal:

> *My Dear Charge,—You solicit me or Captain Harris to advise you as to what next to do. Well, as Harris says he has always had the heft of the load on his shoulders, I will try and respond myself and let Harris rest. Ha! Ha! Well, Marble, we must joke a bit; did we not, we should have the blues, as do you some of those rainy days when you see no living person at the rock…As to the course, you are in the right direction at present. You have one more curve to make before you take the course that leads to the cave.*

The pirate's spirit also told Hiram to be patient:

> *We have a reason for keeping you from entering the cave at once. Moses was by the Lord kept forty years in his circuitous route, ere he had sight of that land that flowed with milk and honey. God had his purpose in doing so, notwithstanding he might have led Moses into the promise, in a very few days from the start. But no; God wanted to develop a truth, and no faster than the minds of the people were prepared to receive it. Cheer up, Marble, we are with you and doing all we can.*

In 1856, Hiram's savings ran out, and he had still not reached the treasure. To finance the digging, he started charging admission to the tunnel and also sold bonds for a dollar that he promised to pay out when he found the gold. To help speed things up, his son Edwin also joined him in excavating the tunnel. By 1864, the tunnel spiraled more than 130 feet down into solid stone.

Thomas Veal and Captain Harris continued through the years to encourage Hiram and Edwin in their digging. They occasionally enlisted the help of other spirits to cheer on the Marbles, like Hiram's deceased best friend C.B. Long, who delivered the following message through a medium: "The names of Hiram and Edwin Marble shall live when millions of years shall, from this time, have passed, and when even kings and statesmen shall have been forgotten."

The Marbles were also encouraged by the local Spiritualist community, who viewed the tunnel as a monument to the power of their faith. Near the tunnel's entrance, they set up a camp of tents and small buildings where they sang, danced and displayed objects they said had been discovered during the excavations. Among them were an ancient sword and a pair of scissors, which the faithful Spiritualists claimed had belonged to the pirates. A skeptical observer thought otherwise: "That they were left there by pirates, years on years ago, no sane man can for a moment believe. The probabilities are that someone deceived Mr. Marble."

Hiram built a house on top of Dungeon Rock and lived there with his daughter and Edwin. On November 10, 1868, after digging for more than sixteen years, Hiram Marble died at the age of sixty-five. After a Spiritualist funeral in which Hiram was interred in the ground near Dungeon Rock, Edwin went back to work and continued tunneling. Spurred on by the spirits, Edwin dug for another twelve years before dying in 1880. He, too, was buried near the rock.

FROM NATURE & ON STONE BY C.A.MALLORY.

According to traditional accounts, there formerly existed a cave in this place, which was freque earthquake of 1658, which closed the original entrance, no vestige of the cave is discernable; and Thomas Veal, was imprisoned alive, hence the place is called "Pirate's Dungeon." It is believed by there,—and various attempts have been made to force an entrance to the cave." Some years ago a p up the place, but succeeded only in displacing a large mass of rocks. Subsequently Jesse Hutchins under the direction of a "Clairvoyant," tried to reach the cave, but he soon abandoned an undertak Hiram Marble, under the guidance of "Clairvoyants" and "Spiritual Mediums," commenced the pre cies; he has penetrated into the solid rock, to a distance of nearly one hundred feet, makin in diameter. He professes to be guided in his operations by the spirits of the pirates, (who occupied Spiritual Media. Should he verify the predictions of the Spirits, in finding the cave and the treasures evidence of the truth of Spiritualism—but should he fail so to do, we shall have proof of wonderful on the part of the excavator.

Hiram's daughter continued to live on top of Dungeon Rock after her father and brother died, and she charged visitors a quarter to enter the tunnel. A sign at the tunnel's entrance read, "Ye who enter here, leave twenty-five cents behind." The area was later given to the city as a park and is now part of Lynn Woods Reservation. Unlike visitors in the nineteenth century, today there's no admission charge to go into the tunnel. It's sealed off with an iron door that's open only on certain days, so be sure to check with the park's website before visiting. Bring a flashlight because it's very, very dark. You might also want to bring a sweater. We visited it on a scorching hot August day, and it was so cold at the bottom of the tunnel that we could see our breaths. After you leave the tunnel, you'll also see an old chimney, which is all that is left of the Marbles' house.

Visiting Dungeon Rock raised certain questions in my mind. The most obvious is: why didn't they stop digging? It seems obvious to me they were never going to find

Nineteenth-century memorabilia from Dungeon Rock. *Library of Congress, Prints and Photographs Division.*

any treasure, and I think it was pretty obvious to almost everyone back then except the Marbles. I'm sure that after digging fruitlessly for so many years, even they must have had some doubts. They never expressed any doubt openly, but they did change the reason they were digging over time. Initially, Hiram started digging to find the treasure, but as the years went on, he later said finding the treasure was just a secondary goal. The main goal was to build a monument to Spiritualism. If that was his intent, he did succeed. The tunnel he dug into Dungeon Rock will probably last for millions of years, so the spirits were right on that account.

The other question that comes to mind is: were there really any spirits involved? I suppose the easiest answer is to say the Marbles were duped by the mediums they consulted and that no spirits were involved at all. However, the Marbles' failure to find treasure doesn't *necessarily* mean the spirits were fake. If you believe in spirits, I think it's plausible to say that a dead pirate's ghost would not be a trustworthy advisor. Pirates make their living by murdering, stealing and lying; why would Thomas Veal change his ways after death? Perhaps he was playing an elaborate joke on Hiram Marble. Spending eternity trapped under a rock must get pretty boring. It's also possible that it wasn't really Thomas Veal's spirit guiding the Marbles at all but some other nameless and ultimately malevolent entity.

Folklorist Joseph Citro says that strange lights are sometimes seen near Dungeon Rock, and he speculates that they're either Thomas Veal trying to entice another poor sucker or the Marbles trying to warn people away. Either way, when you visit Dungeon Rock, leave the Ouija board at home. You don't want to be tricked into digging a tunnel for twenty-five years.

# DEVILISH PLACES

There are more than 110 places in New England that have the word "devil" in their name. That list doesn't even include places that have the words "Satan" or "hell" in their names, just those specifically with the word "devil." Clearly, the Evil One was very active in this area at one time—or at least people thought so.

Why are so many places named after the devil around here? One theory is that many of the locations the English settlers named after the devil were originally connected with local Indians. The English thought the Indians were heathens, and heathens worshipped the devil; therefore, Indians worshipped the devil, and the places they frequented were named to reflect this. Now, of course, the Indians didn't really worship the devil, but the English settlers erroneously believed otherwise.

Another possibility is that when the English encountered New England's abundant weird rock formations, they assumed they were created by some supernatural entity. They weren't aware that retreating glaciers had scoured the earth and dropped thousands of boulders across the landscape. Other than the devil, the only other supernatural entity that could have done it was God, and they couldn't believe that God would have made such inhospitable natural features.

The North Shore is blessed (or cursed) with several of these devilish locations. For example, a rocky promontory on Nahant's coast was called the Devil's Pulpit, or sometimes just Pulpit Rock. Connected to the mainland by a small, natural rock bridge, this unusual and dramatic boulder was popular with painters and photographers for much of the nineteenth and twentieth centuries. Unfortunately, the Devil's Pulpit was destroyed in 1957 by a massive winter storm. Up the coast on Cape Ann, another coastal rock formation called the Devil's Den still survives in Rockport.

Newbury is home to another Devil's Den. Located inland, this den is a small cave in a former limestone quarry. The quarry itself is called the Devil's Basin, and a rock that stands in the basin is called the Devil's Pulpit. That's a lot of devilish activity in one place!

The quarries were first discovered in the late 1600s but were abandoned when more productive quarries were found elsewhere. By the early 1800s, they were popular spots for picnickers. As John James Currier notes in his book *Ould Newbury: Historical and Biographical Sketches*:

> *Pleasure parties were accustomed, during the summer months, to seek rest and recreation there, beguiling the time with marvelous stories in which the Prince of Darkness was given a conspicuous place. In later years the young and credulous found traces of his Satanic Majesty's footsteps in the solid rock, and discovered other unmistakable signs of his presence in that locality; and ever since the Devil's Den, the Devil's Basin, and the Devil's Pulpit have been objects of peculiar interest to every native of old Newbury.*

Three eerie-looking poplar trees grew near the Devil's Den, and young boys who ventured near the cave in the 1800s regarded them warily. If the trees were spooky, the den itself was considered to be downright terrifying, and no one dared to enter it without being properly initiated. The initiation ritual was as follows. Anyone who wished to enter the cave would have to climb to the top of the nearby Devil's Pulpit boulder, where he would repeat certain irreverent phrases he had been taught by friends. Sadly, these phrases, which protected the boys from the evil power that dwelt within the

The devil's footprint in Ipswich. *Photo by author.*

cave, were not recorded and haven't survived to the present. The initiation provided only limited protection because, even after reciting the appropriate words, boys could enter the Devil's Den only in groups. They believed that written on the floor of the cave was a secret name that would kill anyone who entered alone.

In addition to limestone, the cave was also known for interesting mineral deposits of serpentine and soft, gummy chrysotile, a naturally occurring form of asbestos. According to George Lunt's 1873 memoir *Old New England Traits*, he and other boys would often chew the chrysotile, so I hope the irreverent phrases protected them not only from the devil but also from cancer. The Devil's Den is on land that is currently privately owned, so unfortunately it is not easily visited.

However, in Ipswich you can visit the devil's footprint, which he left on a rock as he fled town. According to legend, many years ago, the devil had taken up residence inside a mirror that was located inside Ipswich's Congregational church. The mirror hung behind the pulpit, and during Sunday meetings, the devil could peer over the minister's shoulder and plan evil temptations for the members of the congregation.

The devil was pretty happy in Ipswich until September 30, 1740. That was the day George Whitefield came to town. Whitefield was a passionate Methodist minister from England who had come to America to spread the Gospel with his powerful, fiery preaching. On the morning of September 30, he was preaching to a large crowd on Ipswich's town green, which was across the road from the Congregational church.

At first, the devil just remained inside his mirror. He could hear Whitefield's preaching, but the Evil One was used to listening to preachers talk. Whitefield became more animated and energetic as he talked, and the devil started to get annoyed. He put his fingers in his ears, but soon Whitefield was preaching in a holy frenzy, and the crowd reacted with loud enthusiasm. The devil couldn't take it anymore! He burst out of the mirror, flung open the doors of the church and charged across the green right toward Whitefield.

The devil was huge, hideous and hellishly angry, and the townspeople scattered as the fallen angel raced toward the minister's makeshift pulpit. But George Whitefield didn't even flinch. He stood his ground, and when the devil reached him, the two engaged in hand-to-hand combat.

Whitefield fought the devil back across the town green and into the church, preaching the Gospel as he did. The devil punched, kicked and clawed at the Methodist preacher, but to no avail. Whitefield was filled with the Holy Word and felt no pain.

*Opposite*: An antique postcard of Ipswich's First Congregational Church. A newer building now stands in its place. *Boston Public Library.*

*Right*: An eighteenth-century engraving of George Whitefield by Elisha Gaudet. *Library of Congress, Prints and Photographs Division.*

GEORGE WHITEFIELD.M.A.

*Elisha Gallaudet*                    *Sculp: NYork.1774*

The two fought their way up the church steeple and onto the roof. The townspeople watched in horror as they wrestled back and forth, until finally, with a holy shout, George Whitefield flung the devil off the roof to ground below. The devil landed on one foot and sprang away across the horizon in terror, never to be seen in Ipswich again.

When the devil hit the ground, he left his footprint in a rock, which can still be seen today. The rock with the footprint is located in front of the First Church in Ipswich at 1 Meetinghouse Green. The footprint is helpfully circled with green paint so you can't miss it.

Although you may or may not believe in the devil, George Whitefield was an actual person, one of the founders of the Methodist movement in the

1700s. An Englishman who was famously cross-eyed, he traveled to America three times to preach and became good friends with Benjamin Franklin. Whitefield's influence is still felt today at Christmas when people sing "Hark! The Herald Angels Sing," a carol he co-wrote with John Wesley. Whitefield died on September 30, 1770, in Newburyport, thirty years after his famous battle with the devil in Ipswich. His body is buried in a crypt underneath the pulpit of Newburyport's First Presbyterian Church.

# Witch Rock

Since the devil made his mark on the local landscape, we shouldn't be surprised to find that witches left their marks as well. There are several places named after witches on the North Shore, but one of the most unusual was found in Danvers in 1978.

In the fall of that year a group of archaeologists surveying the town of Danvers discovered a large boulder painted with occult symbols in a forest near Route 128. These symbols, or pictograms, had been painted in black paint and were quite faded. After the archaeologists tested the paint, they found it was not modern industrial paint but was instead composed of hematite and a binder of egg albumin or casein, a milk protein. The paint was quite old. In other words, pranksters or modern occultists had most likely not painted these symbols.

If not, where had they come from? One possible explanation is that the symbols were painted in 1692 during the Salem witch hunt. Danvers was originally Salem Village, the epicenter of the witch trials, and the boulder stands near where accused witches John and Elizabeth Proctor once lived. It's possible that the symbols were painted to ward off evil.

An examination of the symbols themselves suggests they were painted later than the 1690s, though. The symbols include an upside-down pentacle (a five-pointed star encompassed by a circle), a caduceus (a symbol of the planet and Roman god Mercury) and a symbol that is a combination of the astrological sign for Aries and the Archepiscopal cross, which has two horizontal arms rather than one. Although these magical symbols have been around for centuries, there is no historic evidence that they were ever painted on rock in New England during the seventeenth century.

If they weren't painted during the witch trials, when were they created? It's possible they were created during the witch trial bicentennial in 1892,

A diagram of the symbols painted on Witch Rock. *Illustration by Onix Marrero.*

when the area was gripped by an increased interest in its dark history, or perhaps by practicing occultists who lived after the 1600s.

At this point, no final explanation for the mysterious pictograms has been found. The area near the boulder has since been developed for housing. I believe the rock still exists, but it may now be on private land. More information about its location can be found in Salvatore Trento's *Field Guide to Mysterious Places in Eastern Northern America*, but please don't trespass!

# BEVERLY'S WITCHES WOODS

In the town of Beverly, there's a large wooded conservation area officially called Beverly Commons, but it's also been known for many years as Witches Woods. Many people claim the area got that name because accused witch Giles Corey hid in these woods while he was trying to escape from the Salem witch trials. I'm not sure how true that story is. Giles Corey was quite elderly when he was accused of witchcraft, and although it's a short trip now, it wasn't easy to get from Salem Village to Beverly back in the 1600s. Still, it's a good story, and there could be some truth to it.

Even better stories about Witches Woods can be found in Caroline Howard King's *When I Lived in Salem, 1822–1866*. This book is a fascinating collection of reminiscences about daily life on the North Shore in the early nineteenth century. Do you want to know what people ate for dessert in 1836? Marlborough pudding and cranberry pie, of course. What happened to a woman if she fell asleep during the interminable Sunday church services? A church official called the tidy man (aka the tithing man) would tickle her

Thisselwood, the Beverly summer home of Caroline King Howard. *The Schlesinger Library, Radcliffe Institute, Harvard University.*

awake with a foxtail mounted on a pole. Drowsy men weren't treated so gently—they were whacked back into consciousness with a wooden knob mounted on the other end.

Caroline Howard King's family owned a summer home in Beverly called Thisselwood, which abutted Witches Woods. According to King, the people who lived in Beverly at the time were quite superstitious. She writes, "When we first went to the Beverly Shore, in 1840, the country people were a very primitive and unsophisticated race." The door of each house was protected against evil by a horseshoe hung over it, and the corners of the house were decorated with the same. An elderly African American woman who lived in the neighborhood was believed to be a witch and was said to posses the evil eye.

The locals also believed that a headless ghost wandered through the woods. They were reluctant to speak of him, but many people had seen him walking forlornly among the trees with his head under his arm. No one was able to tell Caroline what had led the ghost to his unfortunate fate. Caroline King and her family jokingly named him Heady, but she confesses that she didn't laugh on late-night carriage rides through the woods. She was actually quite afraid of seeing Heady.

She never did see the decapitated ghost but instead had another odd experience in Witches Woods. It's a slightly unsettling story.

One pleasant summer morning in 1841, Caroline (who was nineteen at the time) set off for a stroll in Witches Woods with her nine-year-old cousin, Nony, and a maid named Lucy Anne. After walking through the forest for a while, they decided to rest and have a snack under some hemlock trees a short distance from the path. After they finished eating, they walked back to the path—but it wasn't there. Despite searching in all directions, they couldn't find any path at all. It was if it had vanished.

Caroline and her companions wandered through the woods for hours but somehow always came back to the exact same spot. They could hear the ocean and knew they weren't far from home, but they were unable to get there. It seemed like they were wandering in endless circles.

Lots of people get lost in the woods (I've been one of them), but things were about to get even stranger for the girls. Trying one last time to find the path, they set out through the trees and stumbled on a clearing in the woods. In the middle of the clearing stood the remains of a long-abandoned house: a chimney, a cellar hole and a stone stoop with an enormous lilac bush growing next to it. Caroline knew her neighbors called this ruin the Homestead or the Witch Farm, and they shunned it because it was haunted. It was supposed to sit in the very heart of Witches Woods.

Excited to have at least arrived someplace new, the girls searched around the clearing and saw that a path led up a small hill. They followed it up through the trees until they reached the top of the hill. Once there, they had a view over the woods and could see nearby, at the foot of the hill, a cozy farmhouse with smoke rising from its chimney. It seemed to be in the clearing where they had just been, but for some reason, they hadn't seen it before, which seemed odd. The house had a broad stone stoop just like the ruin, and as they watched, a woman came outside and scattered feed for the chickens. Excitedly, Lucy Anne ran down toward the house to ask for directions home.

Caroline and her cousin waited and waited, and finally a dejected Lucy Anne returned. She said that no matter how many times she had walked around the hill, she couldn't find the farmhouse. In fact, all she saw were "hateful solemn old pine trees." However, she had found a dry streambed, which they followed out of the woods to the beach. From there, they trudged home to Thisselwood.

The writer James Russell Lowell was staying with the King family at the time, and during a previous night's dinner, he had told them he had the second sight. The Lowell family estate in Cambridge was reportedly haunted by the ghost of a British officer who had died there during the Revolution, and James Russell Lowell had seen the ghost late one night. (The Lowell estate is now the campus home of Harvard University's president.)

Convinced that he could find the Witch Farm, Lowell set off determinedly into the woods. After about an hour, he returned to Thisselwood "baffled and disconcerted." He had followed the dry streambed but had been unable to find either the abandoned farm or the thriving, inhabited one. He made several other excursions into Witches Woods that summer, but they were equally frustrating. The mysterious farm could not be found.

James Russell Lowell. *Library of Congress, Prints and Photographs Division.*

Many years later, Caroline King Howard was reading an English newspaper when she saw an article about James Russell Lowell. In the article, titled "Is This a True Story of Lowell?" Lowell tells of a mysterious Witch Farm in America that appears to travelers only once and then can never be seen again. Lowell told the writer that he saw it himself once but that it had vanished when he retraced his steps.

King writes in her memoir:

> *No he never did see it! But it amused me to find that he had taken possession of the story....No it is not a true story of Lowell...but I shall always believe that on that lovely summer morning Nony, Lucy Anne and I were granted a glimpse of the Old Homestead Farm as it looked some other morning one hundred years ago!*

Beverly Commons is conservation land that is open to the public, so you can visit yourself and try to find Witch Farm. Beverly Commons is located just south of Route 128 with entrances on Greenwood Avenue, Common Lane and Branch Lane. If you do find the old farmhouse, I don't recommend going inside. You don't want to vanish along with it.

# DANVERS STATE HOSPITAL CEMETERY

If you grew up in northeastern Massachusetts, you're probably familiar with the Danvers State Hospital. When I was a child, the name of this state-run facility for the mentally ill was completely synonymous with "insane asylum." For example, my brother might say to me, "Stop acting like a weirdo or you'll get taken to Danvers!" I often pictured men in white coats with nets dragging me off, and we thought some of the local eccentrics had spent time at Danvers.

Clearly, we weren't particularly sensitive or politically correct. Mostly we were afraid of being sent to Danvers State Hospital, which loomed as large in our minds as it did over the physical landscape. We used to pass by it on the highway sometimes when heading into Boston or to my grandmother's house. The hospital was a big, gloomy, Gothic, brick monstrosity that sat on top of a hill overlooking the surrounding area. If a Hollywood director were looking for the stereotypical sinister asylum, Danvers Hospital would be it.

It didn't always have a spooky reputation. When Danvers first opened in 1874, it was a state-of-the-art facility and was staffed by the best-trained psychiatrists in the country. There were separate wards for male and female patients and secure wards for the most difficult ones. A vast network of tunnels connected the hospital's different wings so patients and staff wouldn't need to go outside during the winter. At some point, a tunnel was even built to connect the hospital with a steam plant located all the way at the bottom of the hill.

At first, everything functioned smoothly at Danvers State, but over the decades, it became crowded and squalid as the demand for mental care outstripped the available space. The hospital was originally designed to accommodate 450 patients, but by 1939, it had more than 2,300 patients crammed into its rooms. Some were even confined in the underground tunnels. The death rate was quite high. For example, in 1939 alone, 279 people died within the walls of the asylum, a death rate of more than 10 percent.

Rumors began to spread about inhumane treatment and the indiscriminate use of lobotomies and heavy drugs to sedate the patients. Once a beacon for modern psychiatry, the hospital gradually became an embarrassment to the state. As the physical buildings began to decay, its different wards were slowly shut down and the patients moved elsewhere. In 1992, Danvers State was finally closed.

Staff who worked there said it was haunted while it was open, but even more stories about ghosts and supernatural phenomena began to spread after it shut down. Danvers became a popular spot for ghost hunters, and several photographed mysterious orbs of light on the grounds. Due to its imposing architecture and haunted reputation, Danvers was chosen as the setting for *Session 9*, a horror film about men removing asbestos from an abandoned mental hospital. If you want to see what Danvers looked like during the height of its decay, rent *Session 9*. It definitely was creepy! It also seems likely that Danvers was the inspiration for Briarcliff Manor, the haunted Massachusetts sanitarium in the TV show *American Horror Story: Asylum*.

In 2005, the state government sold the facility to real estate developers, who decided to make luxury condominiums and apartments. Despite protests from preservationists, they tore down many of the original buildings, leaving only the central complex. The developers then built several new ones on the site, but they were destroyed by a mysterious fire in 2007. A cause was never determined, and although the site was monitored by multiple video cameras, no one was seen on the night of the fire. Undeterred, the developers rebuilt and eventually opened an apartment complex called Avalon Danvers.

Danvers State Hospital, now the Avalon Danvers apartment complex. *Photo by author.*

Although I'm sure the owners of Avalon Danvers wish they could erase the site's unsavory history, they have acknowledged it in at least one way: they have restored the hospital's cemetery and opened it to the public.

Thousands of people died at Danvers State. Many were buried by their families in cemeteries around the state, but others weren't so lucky. Either their survivors didn't claim their bodies or the staff didn't even know who their families were. These unclaimed bodies were buried in a cemetery on Danvers State's grounds.

Unlike most cemeteries, for efficiency, the graves at Danvers were marked only with numbers, not names. There are hundreds of them—some marked with stone posts and others with small stone plaques. Although the cemetery was once weedy and overgrown, today the grass is mowed and the

Numbered anonymous grave markers in the Danvers State Hospital cemetery. *Photo by author.*

grounds well maintained. In recent years, an advocacy group has tried to identify everyone buried at Danvers, and its members have erected a large monument listing the names they've discovered. Some graves that were once only marked now have names as well.

If you want to visit the Danvers State cemetery, park in the main lot at Avalon Danvers. Facing the main building, walk along the sidewalk to the right. Make sure you're on the side of the street opposite the buildings. You'll eventually come to a path that travels down the hillside to the cemetery. Please be respectful and honor the work the advocacy group has done to bring peace to Danvers's final and permanent residents.

# DOGTOWN COMMON

More than three thousand acres of boulder-strewn forest sit between the towns of Gloucester and Rockport. Situated inside the forest are the ruins of an eighteenth-century ghost town called Dogtown.

Local legends claim that Dogtown was established by people trying to avoid pirate raids or Indian attacks, but historical records indicate it was established by the town of Gloucester in 1721 as a village called the Commons Settlement. When Gloucester was first settled in the early 1600s, a thick old-growth forest filled the area, but over time, the trees were used as lumber. Once the trees were gone, the town fathers opened the area to settlers, hoping to attract new people to Cape Ann.

The Commons Settlement thrived for several years, even though the stony soil was bad for growing crops. Instead of farming, the Commons people worked as blacksmiths, barrel makers and millers. Others cared for sheep and cattle that grazed on the sparse grass that grew on the Commons. But eventually, the Revolutionary War took many Commons men away from home, and the wealthy families who lived near Gloucester Harbor decided to relocate the church closer to the waterfront. Once only a short trip from the church, the Commons Settlement became a distant backwater. The village never recovered from these twin blows, and residents began to drift away. The thriving, industrious settlement became poverty-stricken and filled with crumbling, empty houses. The Commons Settlement became known as Dogtown because there were more stray dogs living there than people.

But a few people did stay in Dogtown, primarily elderly widows. Many were rumored to be witches, like Luce George, Molly Jacobs and Molly Stevens. Molly Jacobs read fortunes and threatened to curse anyone who didn't give her money, while Rachel Rich told the future by looking at coffee grounds. Her daughter Becky also told fortunes but preferred to use tea leaves. Rachel also sold a healing tonic made from fox berry leaves, spruce tops and other local herbs.

Not all the Dogtown witches were as benevolent as Rachel Rich. Luce George had a bad reputation, but her niece Thomazine "Tammy" Younger had an even worse one. Tammy Younger lived in a dilapidated house near the road through Dogtown and harassed and cursed anyone who passed by. The only way to get her to reverse the curse was to give her food or money.

Tammy's reputation as a witch persisted up until her death at the age of seventy-six in 1829. When she died, her nephew ordered a coffin made for her by local craftsman John Hodgkins. Hodgkins's family was used to having

A carved boulder marking the site of Dogtown's former public square. *Photo by author.*

coffins in their home, but the mere presence of Tammy's coffin made them uneasy, even though her body wasn't in it. Mrs. Hodgkin claimed she felt an unnatural chill around the coffin and believed that Tammy's ghost was visiting their house. The eerie feeling stopped only when John Hodgkins moved the coffin into the barn.

In addition to witches, Dogtown was also a refuge for former slaves. A woman named Old Ruth was one of them. Ruth preferred to wear men's clothing, claiming she found them more comfortable for the type of heavy labor she did. However, she also sometimes called herself John Woodman, so there may have been more to her cross-gender behavior than simple comfort. Sadly, Old Ruth was eventually taken to the local poorhouse, where she was made to wear women's clothing. A Dogtown man of English descent named Sammy Stanley also wore clothing of the opposite gender. Sammy had been raised by his mother as a girl, and as an adult, he always wore a woman's kerchief over his head. He found work as a nurse and a launderer, two trades usually practiced by women.

The last person to live in Dogtown was a freed slave named Cornelius Finson. Finson had worked as a hog butcher and a clerk for fishing boats on the Gloucester dock, but he spent his last days digging for treasure in the cellar of Molly Jacobs's abandoned house. In February 1839, he was taken from Dogtown by a constable who found him cold and half frozen in the snow. Seven days after being brought to the Gloucester poorhouse, Finson died.

After Finson's death, Dogtown became a ghost town. The remaining houses either collapsed or were torn down, and the area was used only for grazing cattle and the occasional picnic. The eerie, boulder-strewn landscape, abandoned ruins and tales of witchcraft all combined to give the area the spooky reputation it still has today. Rumors of a possible werewolf (see chapter six) only added to that reputation.

Some people liked the uncanny atmosphere that surrounded Dogtown Common. One of them was Marsden Hartley, the famous twentieth-century American painter. Hartley was born in Maine in 1877 but found his initial fame with paintings he created while living in Europe. He returned to the United States in 1930 and traveled to Cape Ann to paint in the summer of 1931. Depressed over the death of a lover and suffering from multiple ailments, Hartley found solace and artistic inspiration in the desolation of Dogtown. He wrote, "The place is forsaken and majestically lonely, as if nature had at last formed one spot where she can live for herself alone." Hartley had a tendency toward mysticism and felt Dogtown was a place of "psychic clarity." His career gained new focus after painting that summer in Dogtown, and he left feeling refreshed and energized.

Not everyone found Dogtown's desolate beauty quite as inspiring. Among them was Roger Babson, a descendant of one of Gloucester's earliest settlers and a multimillionaire who made his fortune selling financial forecasts.

Roger Babson. *Library of Congress, Prints and Photographs Division.*

Babson, who was born in 1875 and died in 1967, felt that too many people looked at Dogtown and thought of decay, social outcasts and the supernatural. Instead, he thought they should be focused on the hardworking industrious men and women who founded the village. He decided to improve the area, and people's minds, by carving motivational slogans onto some of the large boulders that littered Dogtown.

Although his idea was unorthodox, the people of Cape Ann agreed to it for two reasons. First, the Great Depression (which Babson had accurately forecast) had hit the United States, and unemployed men could be put to work carving the slogans. Second, Babson had agreed to sell five hundred acres of land to Gloucester for a reservoir with the requirement that he be allowed to continue carving the boulders. Fresh water and money in the local economy were more valuable than preserving Dogtown's natural state, and the carved boulders were not the strangest of Babson's ideas. For example, after running a failed presidential campaign, he went on to write a pamphlet called *Gravity—Our Number One Enemy* and create an anti-gravity research center in New Hampshire.

One of the carved Babson boulders in Dogtown. *Photo by author.*

This boulder proclaims the truth in Dogtown. *Photo by author.*

Babson's research center shut down many years ago, but his boulders remain. There are thirty-six of them, and hikers in Dogtown will be inspired, or perhaps just puzzled, by slogans like "USE YOUR HEAD," "INDUSTRY," "SPIRITUAL POWER" and "IF WORK STOPS VALUES DECAY." Rather than dispel the area's uncanny reputation, Babson's boulders just contribute to it. Carved when Dogtown was an area of grassy meadows, the stones are now obscured by the dense forest that has grown up around them. Babson's industry and hard work are being overtaken by Mother Nature.

Dogtown is definitely worth visiting if you're on the North Shore, but I do suggest bringing a friend. The area is very large, the trails are not always clearly marked and the terrain is quite rocky. It's easy to get lost, and you may not see any other people for hours. The isolation is pleasant if you're looking for peace and quiet, but it does bring risks. There have been at least three murders in Dogtown in the last fifty years, and locals also claim that multiple people have simply disappeared there in the past. So if you visit Dogtown, be sure to follow Roger Babson's advice and use your head.

*Chapter 5*

# THREE NORTH SHORE ECCENTRICS

R oger Babson wasn't the only person in the North Shore's history who had some strange ideas. There have been dozens, and here are brief portraits of three men from the area who definitely marched to the beat of their own drums.

## LORD TIMOTHY DEXTER

Although he later proclaimed himself a lord, Timothy Dexter was born in 1747 to humble parents in Malden, Massachusetts. At the age of eight, they sent him to live with a neighboring farmer, and when he turned fourteen, he went to Charlestown to learn the art of making leather.

Despite his early years doing menial work, Dexter always suspected he was destined for better things:

> *I was born when great powers ruled, on Jan. 22, 1747. On this day, in the morning, a great snow storm; the signs in the seventh house; whilst Mars came forward Jupiter stood by to hold the candle. I was to be one great man.*

He took his first small steps toward that destiny when he moved to Newburyport. He opened his own leather-curing business and married a widow who was seven years older than him. She ran a lucrative grocery business from the basement of their home, while he made a good profit from curing hides.

Dexter seemed like your average hardworking American in the early years of his life, but after he invested his and his wife's money in mercantile ventures, his eccentricities began to appear. He had a terrible instinct for the merchant business and made poor decisions, but somehow his bad choices always turned out to be profitable.

For one of his first business ventures, Dexter decided to send a merchant ship full of bed warmers and stray cats to Jamaica. The other Newburyport merchants scoffed at him. After all, Jamaica was warm and tropical. Why would the Jamaicans buy bed warmers? And who wanted a bunch of mangy cats? Dexter had the last laugh, however. Jamaica's main industry was making molasses, and it turned out the bed warmers could easily be adapted into molasses dipping pans. The Jamaicans bought every bed warmer on

the ship, and they also bought the cats. Luckily for Dexter, the island was suffering from a rat infestation at the time.

He invested the profits from the Jamaica trip in other ventures that seemed equally illogical. For example, Newcastle, England, was one of the leading coal producers in the 1700s. Oddly, Dexter decided to send a ship full of coal to Newcastle. Once again, his fellow merchants mocked him, believing that no one would buy it. To their surprise, and Dexter's delight, the English bought the entire boatload. The Newcastle miners were on strike when his ship arrived, and there was in fact a shortage of coal. In another venture, he decided to send a ship of woolen mittens to Jamaica. Once again, luck was

Lord Timothy Dexter's Newburyport home, with wooden statues. *Library of Congress, Prints and Photographs Division.*

with him. Merchants from Asia were visiting the island when his ship arrived and purchased all the mittens to resell in Siberia.

There's some debate whether Timothy Dexter was very lucky or secretly very smart. I suspect both, but he also sought supernatural help when making business decisions. He often consulted Lynn's prophetess Moll Pitcher before sending a ship on a voyage, and he was known to meet with other fortunetellers who lived in Newburyport. Dexter also had his own small collection of occult books about divination and dream interpretation in case the professionals were unavailable.

Regardless of whether he was lucky, smart or helped by supernatural forces, Timothy Dexter soon became the wealthiest man in Newburyport and one of the wealthiest men in Massachusetts. Although he gave money to charity and local churches, Dexter was not humble. He was rich and proud of it.

At one point, he moved to Chester, New Hampshire, where he declared himself that town's king, but in 1798, he returned to Newburyport and purchased a mansion on High Street. This tasteful mansion had been built in 1771 in the classic Georgian style, but once he took possession of it, Dexter added minarets and gilt decorations. The result was something of an eyesore. As one historian wrote, "He caused it to assume a gaudiness and cheapness that was most undesirable to a person of taste."

If his neighbors thought the minarets and gilt were in poor taste, it's safe to say they were downright horrified when he added large wooden statues on the property's wall and in the garden. There were forty statues in total, representing historical figures like George Washington and Napoleon Bonaparte, allegorical goddesses like Fame and Liberty, a small band of Native Americans and four lions. When he finished decorating his house, he declared himself "Lord Dexter, the first in the east, the first in the west and greatest philosopher in the western world."

As befits a lord, Dexter rode around Newburyport in a carriage emblazoned with a baronial crest. His entourage included a powerfully built, tall man named Dwarf Billy and a personal poet, Jonathan Plummer, whose only job was to compose odes praising his lordship. As also befits a lord, Dexter drank heavily and threw lavish parties. One of the most lavish was a mock funeral he held for himself, which included an expensive mausoleum and a mahogany coffin with silver handles. More than one thousand people attended, but the saddest moment actually came after the funeral, when Dexter beat his wife because she hadn't shed any tears. This is just one incident in the long, contentious relationship Dexter had with his wife. He often told visitors to his house that she had died, and when his wife appeared, he would explain that she was just a ghost.

To prove he was a great philosopher, he wrote a book called *A Pickle for the Knowing Ones*. It was almost completely incomprehensible. Here's a sample passage:

> *Ime the first Lord in the younited States of A mercary Now of Newburyport it is the voise of the peopel and I cant Help it and so Let it goue Now as I must be Lord there will foller many more Lords pretty Soune for it Dont hurt A Cat Nor the mouse Nor the son Nor the water Nor the Eare then goue on all is Easey Now bons broaken all is will all in Love Now I be gin to Lay the corner ston and the kee ston with grat Remembrence of my father Jorge Washington the grate herow 17 sentreys past...*

Needless to say, critics hated *A Pickle for the Knowing Ones*. Not only was it nonsensical, they claimed, but it was also entirely lacking in punctuation. In response, Dexter released a second edition that had two additional pages filled only with commas, question marks and periods.

Lord Timothy died in 1806 at the age of fifty-nine, undone by years of heavy eating and hard drinking, and was buried in a modest grave at Newburyport's Old Hill Burying Ground. Shortly after his death, one of the Indian statues at his house fell over, and many other statues were destroyed by a storm in 1815. The remainder was sold at an auction for a fraction of the price Dexter had paid. The house itself still stands on High Street and is once again a tastefully decorated private home.

# John Murray Spear and the New Motive Power

In the last chapter, I told how spirits instructed Hiram Marble to dig the tunnel at Dungeon Rock in 1852. The spirits must have liked the North Shore because, one year later, they told a local minister he would create the new messiah in Lynn.

The minister was John Murray Spear, who was born in Boston in 1804. In the early years of his ministry, Spear was a clergyman in the Universalist Church, worked for the abolition movement and helped run the Underground Railroad in Boston. In 1852, like many other Americans, he began to receive messages from spirits of the deceased. The spirits gave him healing powers and also knowledge that he would otherwise have had no way of knowing. For example, under the guidance of the spirits, he once delivered a series of lectures on geology, a subject he had never studied. Professional geologists who attended were amazed at his accuracy.

In 1853, a group of spirits called the Association of Beneficents told Spear they had big plans for him. The Beneficents included prominent spirits like Socrates, Ben Franklin and Thomas Jefferson, and the group was one of seven spiritual associations that watched over mankind. The spirits gave Spear instructions on how to reform government, marriage, commerce and human society. But before he could reform the world, he needed to build the new messiah. Rather than a being of flesh and blood, the new messiah would be a machine made of metal and powered by magnetism.

The Beneficents instructed Spear to undertake this awesome task in Lynn. A small group of Spiritualists had been living there in a cottage on the high, barren promontory called High Rock, and they had seen visions of angels. These heavenly messengers were a sign that the new messiah would be born on the rock, which was a place of great spiritual power. (Interestingly, the fortuneteller Moll Pitcher had lived and run her business at the foot of High Rock.)

Spear and the Lynn Spiritualists set to work creating the machine, which was known variously as the New Motive Power, the New Motor and the Electrical Infant. They spent more than $2,000 on its component parts,

An antique postcard depicting High Rock tower in Lynn. *Boston Public Library.*

which included metal rods, magnets, wheels and pulleys. The spirits also lent a hand (but sadly, not any money). A group of spirits called the Association of Electrizers controlled Spear's body as he worked on the machine, guiding him in its construction.

After nine months, the New Motive Power was completed. But unfortunately, the mechanical infant, of which no photos or illustrations survive, simply lay inert on a dining room table. Spear and his companions had created its body, but it was not yet alive.

Shortly after the mechanical messiah's creation, a Spiritualist woman in Boston began to suffer what felt like birth contractions. She found this odd, since she wasn't pregnant, but the spirits explained to her that she was giving birth to the spirit that would inhabit the mechanical child. She was rushed to the cottage on High Rock as her contractions increased.

The birth was a success. The woman, whose name was never revealed, knew she had mothered the new messiah. According to one writer of the era:

> *Her own perceptions were clear and distinct that in these agonizing throes the most interior and refined elements of her spiritual being were imparted to, and absorbed by, the appropriate portions of the mechanism—its minerals having been made peculiarly receptive by previous chemical processes.*

As proof, both she and Spear claimed they could feel pulsations of life moving through the machine. The machine didn't move, however, but the spirits indicated that it would after its mother nursed it. The pulsations did increase after nursing, but the mechanical infant still remained inert. No specifics are given about how exactly she nursed the machine.

Spear began to despair, but the Electrizers instructed him to bring the machine to Harmonia, a Spiritualist community outside Kiantone, New York. The spirits said the environment at Harmonia was even more spiritually charged than High Rock, and the infant would thrive there. The Spiritulists of Harmonia welcomed Spear and his metallic child with open arms, but unfortunately, their neighbors in Kiantone and other towns were less open-minded. Learning of Spear's mechanical messiah, they stormed Harmonia and smashed the machine into tiny pieces.

Although the New Motive Power perished at the hands of an angry mob, Spear's dreams of a better world lived on. He traveled across the country supporting the abolitionist cause, started several utopian communities and preached the Spiritualist message in America and England. He died in 1887 and is buried in Pennsylvania.

High Rock, the site of the infant's birth, is now a public park. I'm not sure about spiritual power, but the large stone tower that now stands there has a striking view of the harbor and the Boston skyline. Harmonia, the site of the infant's death, is long gone except for a sulfur spring called Spiritualist Spring. It was uncovered during Harmonia's heyday when the spirits instructed some of the residents to dig a tunnel to find buried treasure and the skeletal remains of prehistoric, web-footed Indians. Much like Lynn's poor Hiram Marble, the excavators found neither gold nor skeletons, but after digging for 150 feet, they did they did strike water. They abandoned their tunnel, but the spring they found still flows today.

## John Hammond, the Master of the Castle

John Hays Hammond Jr. invented many, many things. At one point in his life, he held the most patents of anyone in the United States, surpassing even Thomas Edison. Since his death in 1965, he's now fallen to third place, which is still pretty impressive.

Although not as famous as Edison, many of Hammond's inventions are still in use today. He's probably best known for inventing radio control and once used it to control a yacht that traveled 120 miles without any crew on board. Needless to say, industrialists and the military were very interested in his work. Already born into a wealthy family, Hammond's inventions brought him even greater wealth.

He used this wealth to build what's he most famous for on the North Shore: Abbadia Mare, which is Latin for "abbey by the sea." Known more commonly as Hammond Castle, Abbadia Mare is a medieval-style castle on the Gloucester shore. John Hammond built it as a home for him and his wife, Irene, and they lived there from its completion until their deaths.

Hammond was a rational man of science, but he also had his eccentric side, as you might expect of someone who would build a castle in Massachusetts. Some of his eccentricities are apparent from the castle itself. While much of the building is designed and decorated like an authentic medieval fortress, other parts are just whimsical ideas sprung directly from Hammond's head.

For example, the building has an indoor pool illuminated by a skylight. The pool is flanked by authentic, centuries-old medieval storefronts that Hammond shipped from Europe. Hammond also embedded ancient tombstones in the walls surrounding the pool, and a Roman sarcophagus sits next to the water. I

John Hays Hammond Jr., inventor of radio control and builder of Hammond Castle. *Library of Congress, Prints and Photographs Division.*

suppose the stone crypt was the perfect spot to sit and watch Hammond dive naked into the water from the second-floor balcony, his favorite way to enter the pool.

Also near the pool is a nude statue of Hammond that he commissioned as a gift for his wife. Unfortunately, she hated it. Mrs. Hammond added a fig leaf to it for modesty and placed it outside the castle walls where no one would see it. When the castle became a museum, the statue was moved back indoors, but the fig leaf still remains.

Hammond loved to entertain and held lively, raucous parties. Some guests got more than a good dinner and some lively conversation, though. The doorway to one of the guest bedrooms is covered with wallpaper, so it's indistinguishable from the walls when it is closed. Hammond could control the door remotely and delighted in shutting it when his guests were asleep. When they awoke, they were unable to find their way out of the room. Hammond had a good laugh, but I think the guests must have had panic attacks, particularly if they were claustrophobic.

Like Hiram Marble and John Murray Spear, John Hammond was also interested in communicating with the dead. Hammond added a scientific twist to the methods of Spiritualism. In the great hall of the castle, he constructed a Faraday cage, a boxlike structure that blocks electrical fields from flowing. When he conducted séances, he would ask the mediums to sit inside the box to ensure their messages from the spirit world were not contaminated by energy from the material world. The Faraday cage no longer exists, but visitors to the Hammond Museum can see the large bleached spot on the floor that marks where it stood. They can also see the skull of one of Christopher Columbus's crewmen, which rests in a glass case nearby.

Hammond's experiments contacting the other world may have had a permanent effect on the castle. It's a popular spot for weddings, but many happy brides have reported the same unusual thing happening at their weddings: a mysterious red-haired woman appears briefly at the celebrations and then vanishes. Staff at the museum believe she is a ghost. Strange voices are also sometimes heard echoing through the halls, and the ghost of Irene Hammond has been seen peering out of windows.

Not one to be left out of any fun, Hammond himself may have appeared at the castle after his death. While they were alive, the Hammonds loved cats and always had several in the house. John loved them so much that he often remarked he hoped to be reincarnated as one after his death. His wish seems to have come true—a large black cat mysteriously appeared in the house shortly after he passed away. None of the staff knew where it came from, but they all noticed the strange feline loved to spend its days sitting in John Hammond's favorite chair.

*Chapter 6*

# SCALY MONSTERS, HAIRY MONSTERS AND SPECTERS

O ver its history, the North Shore has seen its share of witches, pirates and eccentrics. But some of its strangest inhabitants might not be human at all.

## THE GLOUCESTER MERMAID

The cold, deep Atlantic Ocean lies just off the North Shore. Although scientists are continually learning more about what lies beneath the waves, there are still many mysteries for mankind to discover. Sometimes those mysteries surface to discover us.

Many years ago, a group of fishermen was sailing across Gloucester Harbor toward the open ocean. As the men headed away from shore, they noticed a large, fish-like object moving just under the surface toward their boat. They thought at first it might be a shark, but as it drew nearer, the men realized it looked like no other fish they had ever seen. It picked up speed as it drew nearer. Just as the mystery creature was about to collide with their boat, it leapt out of the water and landed on the deck.

It was a mermaid. From the waist up, the mermaid looked like a human woman, but her lower parts were those of an enormous fish. Rather than having hips and legs, the mermaid had a long, scaly tale that ended in fins.

An eighteenth-century depiction of mermaids. *Library of Congress, Prints and Photographs Division.*

What would you do if a mythical sea-maiden jumped onto your boat? Would you smile and ask her what life was like under water? Would you scream and run into the cabin?

Personally, if I saw a mermaid, I would probably be paralyzed with amazement but also happy to find that a mythical creature was actually real. Unfortunately, the fishermen weren't either amazed or happy. They were terrified.

While his crewmates cowered in terror, one fisherman grabbed a hatchet and charged at the mermaid. She dove off the side of the boat but clung to it with one hand, looking up at her attacker. Mercilessly, he chopped off her hand. The mermaid sank down into the water. She surfaced once and gave a great sigh and then sank again under the waves. The fishermen did not see her again on their voyage. When the men examined her hand, they found it was identical to a human woman's, even having a woman's fingernails. The mermaid has not been seen since in Gloucester Harbor.

It seems strange for fishermen to attack an unarmed mermaid, but the precedent had been set in New England many years earlier. In the 1630s, English traveler John Josselyn visited Maine. One stormy night in June 1639, he gathered together with some of the local settlers for dinner. As the night went on, they began to tell stories of the strange things they had seen in this new land.

One man, named Mr. Mittin, told how he had seen a triton (or merman) while paddling around Casco Bay in a canoe. The triton grabbed Mr. Mittin's canoe, and Mr. Mittin chopped off the creature's hand. The triton sank under the waves, "dyeing the water with his purple blood, and was no more seen." When Mr. Mittin examined the hand, it was "in all respects like the hand of a man."

The two stories are quite similar. Is the later Gloucester version merely a retelling of Mr. Mittin's encounter? It's impossible to say. I think a more interesting question is: why did Mr. Mittin and the fishermen both feel compelled to attack their marine visitors?

Modern Americans tend to view merfolk as whimsical, legendary creatures. We think of Ariel in Disney's *The Little Mermaid* and other cute images or perhaps even seductive sea-people who want to spend a few hours in a human's company. While people in the past certainly did think of mermaids and mermen as seductive and enchanting, they also realized that, like the ocean itself, they had a dark side.

For example, many legends tell of mermaids who followed ships, hoping to seduce handsome sailors to become their spouses in their undersea homes. The handsome sailors were almost always hesitant to leap from the deck into the mermaids' arms. After all, would they even be able to breathe underwater or would the mermaids drag them to their deaths? Since their chosen mates would not dive into the sea willingly, the mermaids raised storms to sink the

A 1615 engraving of a triton by Jacques de Gheyn. *Wikimedia Commons.*

ships. They saved the handsome sailors and brought them to their homes, but the other crewmen and passengers drowned.

Mermen and tritons are just as aggressive as mermaids when pursuing humans as lovers. Attractive women walking alone on the beach are liable to be snatched away by lustful mermen, a belief that is quite old. Ancient Greek myths tell how Dionysos, the god of wine, defeated a triton that attacked women who were bathing in the ocean before a ritual. Paintings on ancient Greece vases portray the demigod Hercules, the champion of mankind against chaotic forces, battling dangerous tritons as well.

With these legends in mind, I suppose I can understand why the Gloucester fishermen and Mr. Mittin took a "chop first, ask questions later" approach, but I hope if you encounter a merperson, you'll at least ask him what he wants before you break out the hatchet.

# THE DEEP ONES: FACT OR FICTION?

Merpeople aren't the only aquatic humanoids that might be lurking in the waters off the North Shore. A race of fish-like creatures called the Deep Ones resides in a city sunken in the deep water far off the coast. Immortal and powerful, the Deep Ones try to ignore mankind, but if we disrupt them and their habitat, they plan to rise from the ocean and destroy us.

If you think the Deep Ones sound like monsters from a horror story, you're right. They were created by the Rhode Island writer H.P. Lovecraft in 1931 for his short story "The Shadow Over Innsmouth." But in the years since the story was published, many people have wondered if Lovecraft was actually writing about real supernatural entities.

"The Shadow Over Innsmouth" tells the story of a young man from Ohio who comes to Massachusetts to learn more about his family's genealogy. As he explores the libraries and museums of the North Shore, he hears about a decaying coastal town called Innsmouth. People in the neighboring towns shun Innsmouth and speak cryptically of a plague that killed half its population in 1843. They say the citizens of Innsmouth have a distinctive "Innsmouth look": receding foreheads; bulging, unblinking eyes; and oddly creased necks. Further, the town's churches have been shut down and replaced with a cult called the Esoteric Order of Dagon. Despite these ominous rumors, the narrator decides to visit after he sees an oddly shaped gold tiara in a Newburyport museum. The tiara is decorated with images of strange sea creatures and came from Innsmouth.

Innsmouth lies in desolate marshland between Newburyport and Rowley, and when the young man arrives, he finds many buildings deserted and the streets nearly empty. Only young people can be seen; they eye him warily and have the "Innsmouth look." He does glimpse older, misshapen people lurking indoors, including a priest from the Esoteric Order of Dagon wearing a tiara identical to the one in the museum.

Despite feeling a sense of growing dread, the narrator continues to explore the town and encounters a ninety-two-year-old drunkard named Zadok

Allen. Allen doesn't have any strange deformities, and after being plied with a bottle of whiskey, he tells the secret history of Innsmouth.

In the nineteenth century, Innsmouth was suffering through terrible economic times. The fish catch was declining, the mills were failing and the merchant fleet had a run of bad luck. Just as the town seemed doomed, Obed Marsh, one of the town's prominent sea captains, came back from the South Seas with an incredible story. The natives on an island he visited had made an alliance with ancient sea-dwelling creatures called the Deep Ones, who provided the islanders with bountiful catches of fish and gold ornaments from their aquatic city. In return, the islanders simply needed to provide the Deep Ones with human mates—and the occasional human sacrifice.

Obed Marsh proposed that the people of Innsmouth strike a similar bargain with the Deep Ones, who conveniently had an undersea city located near the reef off Innsmouth's coast. In addition to gold and fish, there was another benefit to dealing with the Deep Ones. Children born of the union of a human and a Deep One are born fully human but turn into Deep Ones as they age, growing gills, bulbous eyes and webbed hands and feet. When they are fully transformed, they go to live in the ocean forever, enjoying immortality. While many citizens liked Obed's proposal, others balked at the idea of bargaining with hideous fish-frog monsters. To resolve the issue, Obed and his supporters (with a little help from the Deep Ones) killed their opponents one night in 1843. The Esoteric Order of Dagon took over the churches, and the Innsmouth people began intermarrying with the Deep Ones. Zadok Allen explains that this is why the young people are deformed and the elderly are not seen—nearly everyone in town is descended from the Deep Ones, and as they age, they become fully nonhuman and hide from the public.

The young man is initially skeptical of the old drunkard's story, but after he becomes stranded in Innsmouth and flees through the marshes after dark, he realizes Zadok Allen was telling the truth. As he hides in the marshes, he sees the Deep Ones pursuing him down the road:

> *They were mostly shiny and slippery, but the ridges of their backs were scaly. Their forms vaguely suggested the anthropoid, while their heads were the heads of fish, with prodigious bulging eyes that never closed. At the sides of their necks were palpitating gills, and their long paws were webbed... Their croaking, baying voices, clearly used for articulate speech, held all the dark shades of expression which their staring faces lacked.*

Horror writer H.P. Lovecraft. *Author's collection.*

I won't give away the ending of the "Shadow Over Innsmouth," but I'll just say that sometimes, if you look into your genealogy, you find more than you bargained for.

Lovecraft's tale is clearly fiction, but he did base the fictional decaying coastal community on Newburyport, which he visited in the fall of 1931. Modern-day Newburyport is an upscale coastal community with a quaint downtown and a marina, but the town looked quite different in the earlier part of the twentieth century. Like Innsmouth, Newuryport's economy was failing, and many of the buildings had fallen into disrepair. The downtown business district was almost nonexistent. Lovecraft wrote to a friend that while Newburyport was said "a century and a quarter ago to possess a social life more cultivated & brilliant that that of Washington, [it] is today locally known as the 'City of the Living Dead.'"

"The Shadow Over Innsmouth" was just one of Lovecraft's many stories that tell of horrible, ancient beings waiting to overthrow mankind. Powerful alien beings with unpronounceable names like Cthulhu and Yog-Sothoth and the human cults that support them lurk in the pages of his writings. Again, all of Lovecraft's stories are fictional, but many of his readers have found them so emotionally convincing that they wonder if they might not be based on fact. For example, one of his friends, an amateur writer and occultist named William Lumley, told Lovecraft he believed that his creations were real, a claim Lovecraft laughed off. A female reader who claimed she was descended from the Salem witches offered to reveal the secrets of witchcraft to Lovecraft if only he would share the occult knowledge he was clearly privy to.

H.P. Lovecraft was a staunch atheist until his death in 1937, but after he died, the number of people who believed his fictional works were real grew larger. Multiple versions of the *Necronomicon*, a fictitious book of occult knowledge he concocted for his stories, appeared for sale in the real world, while the Church of Satan wrote and conducted rituals inspired by his writings.

Several occultists have actually conducted magical rituals invoking the Deep Ones. The foremost was Englishman Kenneth Grant, a disciple of the infamous magician Aleister Crowley. Lovecraft based many of his stories on his dreams, and Grant believed the stories are so compelling because Lovecraft accessed true occult entities and dimensions while asleep. Lovecraft thought he was writing fiction, but Grant claims he was actually writing sinister occult truths.

Unfortunately, Grant's rituals with the Deep Ones didn't seem to have very good results. He claimed that during one, a priestess of his occult lodge descended into a water-filled tank, where the Deep Ones appeared and attacked her. Another of his colleagues, a woman named Li, drowned in the ocean; Grant speculated that the Deep Ones played a role in her death.

Here in the United States, the Deep Ones have been magically invoked by Michael Bertiaux, a former Episcopalian priest who is now a prominent occultist. Bertiaux occasionally leads rituals at a secluded lake in the Midwest (possibly Devil's Lake in Wisconsin), which he considers a power zone where the Deep Ones can enter the physical universe. Bertiaux has never publicly described his rituals by the lake, but I hope they were more successful than Kenneth Grant's.

If you're skeptical about the reality of the Deep Ones, you might want to contact the Esoteric Order of Dagon with your questions. An occult order of this name was created in 1980, dedicated to "exploring the connections between the fiction of H.P. Lovecraft and other occult concepts." You can find it online, but its members might not be willing to answer your questions. The group is made up of prominent occultists and is somewhat secretive. There's no word on whether they wear mysteriously shaped gold tiaras.

# The North Shore Sea Serpent

Some other scaly monsters might be swimming with the merpeople and the Deep Ones off the North Shore's coast. Sea serpents have been seen in the area for centuries.

John Josselyn, the English traveler who also wrote about the Casco Bay triton, recorded the first sea serpent sighting in 1639. Off the coast of Cape Ann, one of his Maine neighbors had seen

> a Sea-Serpent or Snake, that lay coiled up like a Cable upon a Rock at Cape-Ann. A Boat passing by with English aboard, and two Indians; they would have shot the Serpent but the Indians dissuaded them, saying that if he were not kill'd outright they would all be in danger for their lives.

Clearly, this was a big animal if the Indians thought it endangered their boat. In 1641, a group of people gathering clams and seaweed on the beach in Lynn saw a similar creature. The sea serpent was as big around as a barrel and fifteen fathoms long. A fathom equals six feet, so the creature was at least ninety feet long! The serpent also appeared again on Cape Ann, where it crawled onto the shore "much to the terror of them that did see him."

The sea serpent stayed clear of the North Shore for most of the eighteenth century, making only a brief appearance in Gloucester in 1793. It must have liked what it found there because, in August 1817, it returned to Gloucester for an extended stay.

The first people who reported seeing the sea serpent that August were laughed at. After all, this was the rational nineteenth century, not the superstitious 1600s. But soon, more and more Gloucester residents saw the creature, including an experienced sailor and two respected townswomen who observed the creature carefully with their telescopes. Eventually, dozens

A nineteenth-century illustration of a sea serpent. *Library of Congress, Prints and Photographs Division.*

of people, both on the shore and in boats, saw the serpent within the course of a few weeks.

The creature was unanimously described as being about the circumference of a barrel and between seventy and ninety feet long. Most witnesses agreed that it was darkly colored and covered in scales, but there were discrepancies in what its head looked like. Some Gloucester residents said it had the size and appearance of a horse's head, while others claimed it looked more like a snake's but much, much larger. Two people also claimed a large horn grew from the creature's head. Many witnesses said the serpent moved through the water with a vertical motion like a giant caterpillar.

The sea serpent was apparently harmless and did not harass the many fishermen and sailors who encountered it in Gloucester Harbor. Still, this didn't stop a ship's carpenter named Matthew Gaffney from shooting at the animal:

> *I had a good gun, and took good aim. I aimed at this head, and think I must have hit him. He turned towards us immediately after I had fired, and I thought he was coming at us; but he sunk down and went directly under our boat, and made his appearance at about one hundred yards from where he sunk.*

The sea serpent was unharmed by Gaffney's shot and continued swimming in the harbor. A few days later, on August 18, an additional serpent arrived, and the two were seen playing in Gloucester Harbor.

Word of the sea serpent spread to Boston and caught the attention of the Linnaean Society of New England. The Linnaean Society had been formed in 1814 to promote the study of natural history, and its members were eager to learn more about the sea serpent. They sent one of their members to Gloucester to collect testimony and hoped to add a specimen to the museum they were creating in Boston.

In September, they got their chance. A young boy walking along Loblolly Cove in Rockport found and killed a strange-looking snake lying on the rocks. Although the animal was only three feet long, it had mysterious lumps along its body and was unlike any other snake he or his family had ever seen. No one in town had ever seen anything like it, either, and people began to speculate that it was a young sea serpent. Two of the adult creatures had been seen swimming together in August, so it seemed likely they had spawned.

The specimen was sent to Boston, where members of the Linnaean Society proceeded to dissect it. Although the creature was in some ways similar to the common black snake found throughout New England, the Linnaean Society declared it was indeed a very young sea serpent. It published an official report and excitedly named the new species *Scoliophis atlanticus*, which is Latin for "Atlantic humped snake."

The society's excitement was short-lived. Upon examining the specimen, three Harvard biologists declared that *Scoliophis atlanticus* was really just a common black snake that had become deformed. The Linnaean Society disbanded shortly afterward in embarrassment.

However, the sea serpent was seen again near Gloucester the following summer, and a hunt was organized to bring it in. After several men failed to capture the creature (one whaler reporting that his harpoon could not even pierce the creature's hide), a captain named Richard Rich claimed he had killed the sea serpent. Crowds gathered in Gloucester to see the monster's body, but when Captain Rich exhibited his trophy, it was obvious to everyone that it was simply a very large horse mackerel. People left angry and disappointed.

Even though many people began to think the sea serpent had been just a hoax, the creature ignored public opinion and continued to make appearances along the North Shore for another two centuries. Later in the nineteenth century, the serpent was seen swimming off the coasts of Nahant,

Lynn, Newburyport, Marblehead, Ipswich and Gloucester. Although seen less frequently in the twentieth century, the serpent still made appearances off Swampscott, Cape Ann, Nahant, Manchester and Marblehead. It was last seen off Gloucester on July 7, 1960.

What has been swimming off the North Shore for over three hundred years? Since no specimen has ever been found, there's no definitive answer. Skeptics have claimed the serpent was everything from a whale entangled in fishing floats to leatherback turtles. Believers have rebutted these arguments, claiming that undiscovered life forms may still lurk deep in the ocean and that experienced sailors and fishermen would have recognized common sea creatures like whales and turtles. I suppose the question won't be settled until the sea serpent once again raises its scaly head above the waves.

## THE DOGTOWN WEREWOLF

The full moon was rising on March 17, 1984, as David Myska walked along Crane's Beach in Ipswich. David was visiting from Boston to do some sightseeing, but when he traveled up to Ipswich that day, I'm sure he didn't plan to see what might have been a werewolf.

David was so shaken by what he saw that he went to the police. He told the Ipswich police he had seen a large, shaggy animal roaming across the tops of the dunes. He claimed, "It was a very large dog or cat, possibly a mountain lion." The local authorities dismissed the possibility that it was a mountain lion, a species that hadn't been seen for two hundred years anywhere in New England, let alone along the North Shore. The animal control officer for Ipswich suggested it might have been a coyote, but David said the animal was too big to be a wolf or coyote.

David Myska's sighting might have been dismissed as a one-time anomaly, but the next night, people in Rowley also reported seeing a large, unidentifiable animal prowling around. On March 23, a deer was found dead in Crane's Beach reservation. Its throat had been slashed, and it had deep fang marks on its neck and body, yet none of it had been eaten. Harry Leno, the Ipswich animal control officer, thought the culprit might be a pack of dogs, one very large dog or perhaps even a wolf. He didn't address where a wolf might come from since they have been extinct in New England for almost as long as mountain lions.

On the night of March 23, two teenagers in Gloucester saw what might have killed the deer. The two were sitting in a parked car on Raynard Street when they saw a large animal run down the road past them. They reported that it was a "gray, monstrous, dog-like animal, running into the woods. It had big teeth and was foaming at the mouth." Raynard Street dead-ends into the unpopulated woods of Dogtown.

Robert Ellis Cahill, a collector of local folklore and a one-time sheriff of Salem, noted that a large animal could easily live in Dogtown and travel to Crane's Beach and Rowley by swimming across the Annisquam River. Cahill also speculated that this large animal might actually be a werewolf.

As with so many supernatural and paranormal entities, the evidence is tantalizingly suggestive but not conclusive. For example, Cahill claimed that the local Indians who originally inhabited Dogtown believed they were descended from a race of dog-headed humanoids. According to Cahill, these same Indians also believed that if anyone from their tribe ate the wolf bane plant, he would assume the form of their ancient ancestors: hairy, clawed and dog-headed. I haven't found this story in my research, and sadly Cahill didn't cite a source for it.

Cahill also notes that wolves plagued Cape Ann's first English settlers. The wolves lived in dens in the Dogtown highlands and came down to devour the fish the settlers were drying on the beach. Furthermore, one of the Dogtown witches named Daffy Archer wore a three-inch wolf's tooth on a necklace around her neck. (Perhaps even more terrifying, Daffy Archer made and sold a medicinal elixir from snail mucous!) Several Dogtown residents were also rumored to have unusually long canine teeth.

A strange animal that might have been a werewolf was seen in Dogtown in 1879. An elderly man named Amos Pillsbury was walking through Dogtown one night and gave the following report:

> *It was a terrible big critter, as big as Brindle's calf. Its eyes were like fire coals, and it ran past me through the bushes, about a rod from the road, with every hair whistling like a bell. It must have been the wolverine—my old granny used to keep us young 'uns quiet with stories about the wolverine out beyond in the woods.*

Amos Pillsbury did not use the word wolverine in our modern sense to describe the weasel-like animal that lives in northern climates but instead used it to describe something wolfish (and quite large). A group of men searched through the woods to find Pillsbury's monster but were unable to locate it.

All that remains of this Dogtown house is its cellar hole. *Author photo.*

Cahill also suggests that a famous incident in Dogtown's history can actually be interpreted as a werewolf attack. In 1891, a local sailor named James Merry wrestled a bull to the ground. Merry was powerfully built and over six feet tall and was obsessed by the bullfights he had seen on a voyage to Spain. One night, Merry and some of his friends were drinking in Gloucester when the topic of bullfighting came up. Someone mentioned they had seen a young bull in a pasture near Dogtown and dared Merry to wrestle it. Merry accepted his dare, and the group of drunken men staggered down the road to the pasture. Despite being very drunk, Merry was triumphant and wrestled the bull to the ground. The spot where this happened in 1891 is still marked with a stone inscribed, "First Attack."

Apparently, one bullfight wasn't enough for James Merry. One year later, on the night of September 10, 1892, he once again made his way to the pasture to wrestle the same bull. He went alone, which perhaps was his fatal mistake. If he had been with friends, they would have reminded him that bulls grow quickly. The young bull he had defeated the year before was now hundreds of pounds heavier.

SCALY MONSTERS, HAIRY MONSTERS AND SPECTERS

Merry's corpse was found in the pasture the next morning. His body had been gored by the bull's horns, but oddly his throat had been slashed open. Friends who saw the wound didn't think a bull had made it, and superstitious people remarked that the moon had been full on September 10. Had he been killed by a Dogtown werewolf? Whatever the answer is, a stone with the words "James Merry Died, September 10, 1892" marks the spot where he perished.

As I mentioned earlier, the evidence is certainly not conclusive, but it is very suggestive. Let's face it: Dogtown and the North Shore in general would make a good place for a werewolf to live. There are plenty of woods and open beaches, and historically, there is an association between werewolves and witches. The boundary between the two is blurry at best. Witches have the ability to transform into animals, including wolves, and both witches and werewolves were believed to be threats to society. Since Dogtown was inhabited by witches, it makes sense for werewolves to live there as well.

Whether Cahill's theory is correct, it seems to be growing in popularity. In the fall of 2013, I went to the Gallow's Hill haunted house/theater in Salem to watch a play based on local legends. During the performance, one of the actors told the audience that the dogs that prowled through Dogtown had actually been werewolves the witches used as guards. As he delivered this speech, a statue of a dog on stage came to life. Its eyes lit up, and it growled at the audience. Is the Dogtown werewolf real? I can't really say, but everyone in the audience was scared.

# BIGFOOT ON PLUM ISLAND

April 11, 1978, was a warm but cloudy day. Tired of hanging around their parents' houses, four local teenagers decided to drive out to Plum Island to enjoy the scenery. They saw more than they bargained for.

The four drove to the Parker River Wildlife Refuge, which is on the southern part of the island. The refuge is composed of more than 4,500 acres of pristine marshes, forests and beaches. Deer, ducks and other wildlife call the area home, as do ferocious greenhead flies in the summer.

On that April day, the teenagers didn't see any wildlife at all. At first, they didn't notice. They were too busy walking along the paths, climbing the observation tower and enjoying one another's company. But after a while, while they were sitting up in the tower, they noticed how quiet it was. They didn't hear any birds. They didn't hear any other people. The only thing they heard was a strange clicking sound, which seemed to be coming from somewhere nearby.

The four teens continued to sit up in the tower. They heard the clicking go on for a while, and then it abruptly stopped. That's when they started hearing the shrieks.

Like the clicks, the shrieks were coming from somewhere close to the tower. They were high pitched and came in short bursts. They weren't made by a human crying out for help but sounded like they were made by something else. But what, exactly? They could have been coming from a large animal, but the four teenagers still couldn't see anything nearby. The shrieks certainly didn't sound like anything the four had ever encountered before.

By this point, the teens decided it was time to leave, and they hurried back to their car. As they drove off down the road, the two boys seated in the front saw something emerge from the bushes and run across the road:

> *The figure that crossed was huge, 7 feet or more, very wide, all black from head to toe. It was a little hunched forward as it walked upright. I noticed its arms were longer than average and they swung as it walked. It took only three steps to cross the road.*

As quickly as it appeared, the creature disappeared into the bushes on the other side of the road.

They stopped the car, and when they got out to investigate, the teenagers could clearly see where the bushes had been trampled down on both sides of the road. They could have followed the trail but wisely chose not to.

As in so many bigfoot sightings, the creature provides only a brief glimpse of itself, as if to say, "Here I am!" before vanishing into the wilderness. People have been seeing similar large, hairy humanoids throughout New England for hundreds of years. Early settlers called them wildmen, after the mythological beings said to haunt medieval Europe's forests. Contemporary New Englanders are most likely to call these creatures "bigfoot" or "sasquatch," two terms from the West Coast that were popularized across the country by mass media.

I suppose it might be possible for large humanoids to be living undiscovered in the vast forests of the Pacific Northwest (or even Maine), but densely populated towns that have been settled for hundreds of years surround Plum Island. Even if bigfoot could find enough food in the Parker River Wildlife Refuge, it seems unlikely that he would remain undiscovered until 1978.

However, bigfoot is sometimes seen in conjunction with other strange phenomena like UFOs or poltergeist activity, leading some paranormal investigators to suggest the hairy humanoids are not entirely of this earth. Some psychics also claim that they have telepathically been in contact with bigfoots and that they are extra-dimensional beings. While these speculations might be a little far-fetched for some people, think about this: in many bigfoot sightings, the creatures are preceded by the smell of rotten eggs. In folklore, the devil and his demons reek of sulfur, which smells just like rotten eggs. This isn't to say that bigfoot is a demon from hell but rather that the humanoid's appearance shares traits with supernatural phenomena reported for thousands of years. And the North Shore has certainly seen its share of supernatural phenomena!

# THE GLOUCESTER SPECTERS

In 1692, the people of Massachusetts Bay felt like their colony was under assault by demonic forces. Dozens of witches were being discovered during the Salem witch trials, while French Catholics and heathen Indians harassed the colony's borders and raided settlements. In the summer of that year, the demonic forces increased their scope and attacked Gloucester, particularly a man named Ebenezer Babson.

At first, Ebenezer Babson didn't realize anything supernatural was happening to him and his family. For several nights, they had heard people running around outside their house but thought little of it. Perhaps it was just neighbor children playing hide-and-seek, because Ebenezer never saw anyone when he went outside in the darkness.

One night, while returning late from town, Ebenezer caught his first glimpse of the troublemakers. As he neared home, he saw two men emerge from his house and run into a cornfield. When he went inside, he asked his family who the men were and was told that no one had visited that night. Thinking this a little odd, Babson went out into the cornfield to find the men. When they caught sight of him, they ran off into a small swamp, saying, "The man of the house is come now, else we would have taken the house!"

Thinking that perhaps the French were preparing to attack Gloucester, Ebenezer and his family ran to a nearby fortified garrison house. Ebenezer brought his gun. That night, they once again heard people running nearby and saw two men lurking in the darkness.

The same pattern continued for several days. The Babson family, joined by some neighbors, stayed inside the garrison. They caught occasional glimpses of strange men running back and forth outside, but more often they just heard them. One night, unseen hands threw stones against the side of the building. The strange men never attacked the garrison, which seemed a little odd. If they were really French invaders, wouldn't they have fired at the Gloucester residents or set fire to the garrison?

Ebenezer Babson realized on July 14 that he and his neighbors were facing something far weirder than a French raiding party. That afternoon, Ebenezer saw six of the strangers outside the garrison house. Rushing outside with their guns, Ebenezer and several other Gloucester men attacked the strangers. Ebenezer raised his rifle to shoot two of them, but his weapon misfired. The men ran into the corn, and Ebenezer pursued them.

Coming up behind three of the men, including one in a white waistcoat, Ebenezer fired his rifle. All three men fell to ground, apparently dead. Ebenezer cried out, "I have killed three! I have killed three!" and ran over to the bodies.

To his amazement, the three men rose up from the ground, completely uninjured. One of them fired a gun at Ebenezer, and then the three ran into the swamp. Ebenezer and his neighbors followed. Once again, Ebenezer shot one, but when he went to where the man had fallen, the man had disappeared. Puzzled by the strange behavior of their foes, the Gloucester men continued to search the nearby area:

> So they all searched the corn; and as they were searching, they heard a great discoursing in the swamp, but could not understand what they said; for they spoke in an unknown language. Afterwards, looking out from the garrison, they saw several men skulking among the corn and bushes, but could not get a shot at them.

The strange men continued to terrify the people of Gloucester throughout July. But they also puzzled Ebenezer Babson and his neighbors. Who were these men? Initially, it was thought that they were French troops and their Indian allies. Some of them looked like they might be French troops, and at least one was described as looking "like an Indian, having on a blue coat, his hair ty'ed up behind." But others looked more unusual, like one who wore "a blue shirt, and white breeches, and something about his head" or a man with bushy black hair seen running through the woods. But if they were French troops, shouldn't they be speaking French? Sometimes the strangers were heard conversing in English; at other times, they spoke in a strange language no one knew—but never in French.

Their behavior was equally as puzzling as their identities. Although it was assumed they were there to invade Gloucester, they never actually harmed anyone or damaged any property. The strangers did shoot at Ebenezer Babson more than once, but each time they missed him. Sometimes the strangers just acted oddly. For example, two Gloucester men named Richard Dolliver and Benjamin Ellery saw a group of the strangers circling an empty house. One of the men struck the house repeatedly with a stick, making a loud noise.

Dolliver and Ellery shot at them, and they disappeared into the woods unharmed, which was another puzzling thing about the strangers. The Gloucester men, no matter how close they were, were never able to harm them. Their rifle shots either missed them, or if they did hit the strangers, they would just get up again and run off. More often the Gloucester men's rifles would jam or misfire, so they didn't even get the chance to shoot.

For example, on July 25, Ebenezer Babson went into the woods to look after his cows. While he was there, he saw three of the strangers standing on a rocky hill overlooking the ocean. Crawling through the undergrowth, Ebenezer came within 150 feet of the men. He had a clear shot and fired his gun. The rifle misfired. He tried again, and once again it misfired. It misfired more than twelve times. The strangers came down from the hill and walked slowly toward Ebenezer. One of them carried a rifle but didn't shoot Ebenezer.

*Nor did they take any more notice of him, than just to give him a look; though he snap't his gun at them all the while they walked toward him, and by him: neither did they quicken their pace at all, but went into a parcel of bushes, and he saw them no more.*

When he returned home, Ebenezer tested his gun. It fired successfully.

By the end of July, the citizens of Gloucester put all the puzzle pieces together and decided the strangers weren't really human at all. They were actually some kind of nonphysical specters. This explained a lot. They didn't harm anyone because they weren't solid physical beings, and they couldn't be harmed for the same reason. It also explained why they seldom left footprints, even in muddy soil.

A modern person might think the spectral strangers were the result of mass hysteria caused by the extreme stress the New England colonists were living under that summer. I don't know if that really explains any more than the concept of specters, and the Gloucester settlers actually found the specter explanation reassuring. As Puritans, they knew that the world was full of omens and phantoms, some sent by God as warnings and some sent by the devil as tests. They ignored the spectral strangers once they concluded their families and property were safe. As the Reverend Cotton Mather wrote, "After this, there occurred several strange things; but now, concluding they were but specters, they took little further notice of them." Like a bad dream, the strange specters eventually disappeared and never came back.

Some historians have doubted the specters were real at all and believe that Ebenezer Babson concocted the whole story. For example, James Pringle, author of 1892's *History of the Town and City of Gloucester, Cape Ann, Massachusetts*, claims that Ebenezer "experienced a monopoly of the occurrences." Similarly, James Connolly, in his 1940 book *The Port of Gloucester*, writes mockingly:

> There was a Mr. Babson, otherwise a normal person and of a well-established line, who used to go out shooting witches. He reported shooting several of them, but when he went out to collect their dead bodies they weren't there. There weren't even footprints of them to show. No.

Pringle and Connolly both conveniently ignore the fact that many people in Gloucester other than Ebenezer Babson saw the specters and gave sworn testimony to a governor's council. Something happened in Gloucester that summer, but I don't think we'll ever know exactly what. I'll let Puritan minister Cotton Mather have the last word on this topic. Here's how he summed up the situation in his 1698 book, *Magnalia Christi Americana: Or, the Ecclesiastical History of New England*:

> I hope the substance of what is written will be enough to satisfy all rational persons that Gloucester was not alarmed last summer for above a fortnight together by real French and Indians, but that the devil and his agents were the cause of all the molestation which at this time befell the town; in the name of whose inhabitants I would take upon me to entreat your earnest prayers to the Father of mercies, that those apparitions may not prove the sad omens of some future and more horrible molestations to them.

# BIBLIOGRAPHY

Arrowsmith, Nancy, and George Moorse. *A Field Guide to the Little People.* New York: Pocket Books, 1977.

Baker, Emerson. *The Devil of Great Island: Witchcraft and Conflict in Early New England.* New York: Palgrave Macmillan, 2007.

Ballou, Maturin Murray. *Fanny Campbell, the Female Pirate Captain: A Tale of the Revolution.* New York: E.D. Long and Company, 1844.

Bigfoot Research Organization, Report #6631. Submitted Thursday, July 17, 2003. www.bfro.net.

*Boston Daily Globe.* "That Witchcraft Case. A *Globe* Reporter Visits Ipswich and Learns the Antecedents of Lucretia Brown. 'Puffer' Somebody Else." May 12, 1878.

*Boston Globe.* "Molly Pitcher Predicted Boston's Great Growth." December 11, 1938.

Bragdon, Kathleen J. *Native People of Southern New England.* Norman: University of Oklahoma Press, 1996.

Brooks, Rebecca Beatrice. "History of Danvers State Hospital." historyofmassachusetts.org.

Cahill, Robert Ellis. *New England's Things That Go Bump in the Night*. Salem, MA: Old Saltbox Publishing, 1989.

Capron, E.W. *Modern Spiritualism: Its Facts and Fanaticisms, Its Consistencies and Contradictions. With an Appendix*. Boston: Bela Marsh, 1855.

Citro, Joseph. *Passing Strange: True Tales of New England Hauntings and Horrors*. New York: Houghton Mifflin, 1996.

————. *Weird New England: Your Travel Guide to New England's Local Legends and Best Kept Secrets*. New York: Sterling Publishing, 2005.

Citro, Joseph, and Diane Foulds. *Curious New England: The Unconventional Traveler's Guide to Eccentric Destinations*. Hanover, NH: University Press of New England, 2003.

Citro, Joseph, and Jeff White. *Cursed in New England: Stories of Damned Yankees*. Boston: Globe Pequot, 2004.

Coffin, Joshua. *A Sketch of the History of Newbury, Newburyport, and West Newbury. From 1635 to 1845*. Boston: Samuel G. Drake, 1845.

Connolly, James. *The Port of Gloucester*. New York: Doubleday, Doran and Company, 1940.

Cristofono, Peter. "Devil's Den and Basin, Newbury Massachusetts." www.mindat.org.

Currier, John James. *Ould Newbury: Historical and Biographical Sketches*. Boston: Damrell and Upham, 1896.

Drake, Frederick C. "Witchcraft in the American Colonies, 1647–62." *American Quarterly* 20, no. 4 (Winter 1968): 694–725.

Drake, Samuel Adams. *A Book of New England Legends and Folk Lore in Prose and Poetry*. Boston: Roberts Brothers, 1884.

Duino, Russell. "Utopian Theme with Variations: John Murray Spear and His Kiantone Domain." *Pennsylvania History* 29, no. 2 (April 1962): 140–50.

East, Elyssa. *Dogtown: Death and Enchantment in a New England Ghost Town.* New York: Free Press, 2009.

*Essex Antiquarian* 7, no. 3 (July 1903). www.lordtimothydexter.com.

Fleming, John. "An Encounter with Chicago's Black Magic Theosophic Neo-Pythagorian Gnostic Master." *Neighbourhood News,* 1979. fulgur.co.cuk.

Godbeer, Richard. *The Devil's Dominion: Magic and Religion in Early New England.* Cambridge, UK: Cambridge University Press, 1992.

Goudsward, David. *H.P. Lovecraft in the Merrimack Valley.* New York: Hippocampus Press, 2013.

Gramly, Richard Michael. "Witchcraft Pictographs from Near Salem, Massachusetts." *Historical Archaeology* 15, no. 1 (1981): 113–16.

Guiley, Rosemary Ellen. *The Encyclopedia of Witches and Witchcraft.* 2nd ed. New York: Checkmark Books, 1999.

Hansen, Chadwick. *Witchcraft at Salem.* New York: G. Braziller, 1969.

Harms, Daniel, and John Wisdom Gonce III. *The Necronomicon Files: The Truth Behind the Legend.* Boston: Weiser Books, 2003.

Harpur, Patrick. *Daimonic Reality: A Field Guide to the Otherworld.* Ravensdale, WA: Pine Winds Press, 1994.

Harriman, Frank F. "Dungeon Rock, Lynn." *Bay State Monthly* 1 (1884).

Hobbs, Clarence. *Lynn and Surroundings.* Lynn, MA: Lewis and Winship, 1886.

Hoey, Mary Ellen Griffin. *Moll Pitcher's Prophecies, or The American Sibyl.* Boston: Eastburn Press, 1895.

Hurd, Duane Hamilton. *History of Essex County, Massachusetts: With Biographical Sketches of Many of Its Pioneers and Prominent Men.* Vol. 2. Philadelphia: J.W. Lewis and Co., 1888.

Ipswich Historic Commission. "Jabesh Sweet House, 32 Water Street." www.historicipswich.org.

Jameson, W.C. *Buried Treasures of New England: Legends of Hidden Riches, Forgotten War Loots, and Lost Ship Treasures.* Atlanta: August House, 2008.

Josselyn, John. *An Account of Two Voyages to New England, Made During the Years 1638, 1663.* N.p., n.d.

Lapersitis, Jack "Kewaunee." *The Psychic Sasquatch and Their UFO Connection.* Mill Spring, NC: Wild Flower Press, 1998.

Lecouteux, Claude. *Witches, Werewolves and Fairies: Shapeshifters and Astral Doubles in the Middle Ages.* Rochester, VT: Inner Traditions, 2003.

Lewis, Alonzo, and James Newhall. *History of Lynn, Essex County, Massachusetts: Including Lynnfield, Saugus, Swampscott, and Nahant.* Boston: John Shorely Publisher, 1865.

Lovecraft, H.P. *The Call of Cthulhu and Other Weird Stories.* New York: Penguin Books, 1999.

———. *Selected Letters, 1925–1929.* Vol. II. Edited by August Derleth and Donald Wandrei. Sauk City, WI: Arkham House Publishers, 1968.

Lunt, George. *Old New England Traits.* New York: Hurd and Houghton, 1873.

Mather, Cotton. *Magnalia Christi Americana: Or, the Ecclesiastical History of New England.* N.p., 1698.

Morton, Thomas. *New English Canaan, or New Canaan, Containing an Abstract of New England, Composed in Three Books.* N.p.: Charles Greene, 1632.

*Newburyport Daily News.* "Is There Buried Treasure in Byfield?" September 27, 2007.

Newhall, James Robinson. *Lin: Or Jewels of the Third Plantation.* N.p.: D.C. Colesworthy, 1880.

*New York Times.* "The Prophetess of Lynn. Reminiscences of the Famous Moll Pitcher. Her Method of Playing the Seer—Something About Her Descendants." July 15, 1879.

O'Neill, J.P. *The Great New England Sea Serpent.* Camden, ME: Down East Books, 1999.

Pringle, James R. *History of the Town and City of Gloucester, Cape Ann, Massachusetts.* Gloucester, MA, 1892.

Roach, Marilynne K. *The Salem Witch Trials: A Day-by-Day Chronicle of a Community Under Siege.* Lanham, MD: Taylor Trade Publishing, 2004.

Russell, Howard S. *Indian New England Before the* Mayflower. Hanover, NH: University Press of New England, 1980.

Shattuck, Ben. "The Monstrous Sea Serpent Was Real!" *Salon,* August 10, 2013. www.salon.com.

Simmons, William S. *Spirit of the New England Tribes: Indian History and Folklore.* Hanover, NH: University Press of New England, 1986.

Skinner, Charles M. *Myths and Legends of Our Own Land.* Philadelphia: J.B. Lippincott Company, 1896.

Snow, Edward Row. *Legends of the New England Coast.* New York: Dodd, Mead and Company, 1957.

———. *Pirates and Buccaneers of the Atlantic Coast.* Boston: Yankee Publishing, 1944.

Starkey, Marion L. *The Devil in Massachusetts: A Modern Inquiry into the Salem Witch Trials.* New York: Anchor Books, 1989.

Trento, Salvatore M. *Mysterious Places of Eastern North America.* New York: Henry Holt and Company, 1997.

Waters, Thomas Franklin. *Ipswich in the Massachusetts Bay Colony.* Ipswich, MA: Ipswich Historical Society, 1905.

Whittier, John Greenleaf. *The Poetical Works in Four Volumes.* New York: Houghton Mifflin and Company, 1892.

Williams, Roger. *A Key Into the Language of America.* N.p., 1643.

Woods, William. *New England's Prospect.* N.p., 1634.

# ABOUT THE AUTHOR

Peter Muise was born in Massachusetts and has lived his entire life in New England. He has degrees in anthropology from Bates College and Brandeis University. Local folklore has been his passion for almost twenty years, and he blogs about it weekly at newenglandfolklore.blogspot.com. From his home in Boston, he makes frequent excursions to the North Shore in search of strange places and unusual stories.

*Visit us at*
www.historypress.net
......................................................................
*This title is also available as an e-book*